Lost in Transp*
Memoir of an Unconve*  *Jonor*

By Eldonna Edwa ***

 Happy Reading!

Eldonna Edwards

Books may be purchased in quantity and/or special sales by contacting the publisher, Whole Heart Publications by email at wholeheartpub@gmail.com
Published by: Whole Heart Publications, Avila Beach, CA
www.wholeheartpublications.com
Author website: www.eldonnaedwards.com
Interior Design by: Deborah Bradseth/Tugboat Design
Cover Design by: Deborah Bradseth/Tugboat Design
Editing by: William Braddock
Cover Photos by: William Braddock
ISBN: 9670384-4-8
10 9 8 7 6 5 4 3 2 1
First Edition
Printed in USA

We are all ordinary. We are all boring. We are all spectacular. We are all shy. We are all bold. We are all heroes. We are all helpless. It just depends on the day.

-- Brad Meltzer

For Kathy
And for all of you still waiting…

AUTHOR'S NOTES

Most fifty-four year-olds can't remember where they left reading glasses (dishwasher? linen cabinet?) let alone an exact conversation or what someone wore on a Tuesday three years ago. Any detective will confirm that ten witnesses to the same event will tell ten different stories. This is *my* story. I've done my very best to tell it honestly and fairly, in a way that captures the essence of people and conversations as well as the organic unfolding of occurrences as I remember them. I harvested relevant excerpts from my former blog and in a couple of instances rearranged the precise order of events for clarity's sake. I've also changed a few names and identifying characteristics to protect the privacy of certain people, noted with an astersisk.* The rest of y'all, well, you knew I was writing about you and you trusted me. I am ever so grateful to each of you.

TABLE OF CONTENTS

PART ONE

ONE

Fall 2006

I bumped into Lucy* in the cafeteria as we both found a table where we could grab a bite and study for an afternoon test.

"Hey, Ellie" she said, sliding her lanky body into the seat across from me. "How's it going?"

I'd decided to go by my nickname at school partly because it felt more casual than Eldonna and partly because people invariably end up calling me everything from LaDonna to Eldora to Elvira when I use my given name.

"Pretty good. I'm starving, as you can probably tell from the size of my sandwich and this mountain of coleslaw." Noticing her tiny salad, I wondered if it was her appetite or budget that kept her from ordering more. "But I can't really eat all this. Would you like some?"

I picked up half my sandwich but she stopped me with a wave of her hand.

"No thank you. I'm vegan, actually."

"Oh. Sorry. I mean, not sorry you're vegan, just that I shoved meat at you."

Lucy laughed.

"It's okay, really. I'm not offended by people who eat meat." She pulled a notebook from her canvas backpack and opened it to a page of neatly scribed outlines. "Are you ready for the test today?"

I swallowed a mouthful of dry bread and shook my head.

"Not really. I missed a couple lectures because I needed to work."

"Would you like to copy my notes?" She slid the notebook across the table. "It's pretty general stuff you probably already know at your age." She stopped and looked up at me, her mouth slightly agape. "Oh man, that didn't come out right. I meant because you have more life experience than most of us."

It was my turn to laugh. I figured I'd stand out like a banana in a bowl of grapes at Cuesta Community College. Surprisingly nobody seemed to notice the middle-aged student standing behind them at the register in the cafeteria, strolling past them in the bathroom without stopping to check her mascara, or nodding knowingly as an instructor discussed the Viet Nam war without having read the text. I didn't take it personally when I felt invisible to my fellow students. Thirty years earlier, married and already caring for two children, my reality was very different from theirs. And yet it was all I could do to suppress the daily urge to hug everyone in the classroom just because they were all so damn fresh and on the verge of their young lives.

"Honestly I'm tickled you'd even want to sit with someone old enough to be your mom let alone help me study for a test."

"Dude, you're way cooler than most people your age. And I totally thought you were in your thirties. I love the insights you offer in class."

I was still considering what it meant to be called *dude* when she added, "Plus you're a massage therapist. I think that's awesome."

"Thanks. I feel pretty old next to all of you but everyone's been really friendly and inclusive. I didn't realize how much I've missed being in school."

She poked at her salad, long fingers curled around a clear plastic fork.

"So can I ask you something, Lucy?"

"Sure, what's up?"

"Are you vegan for ethical or health reasons?"

"Both I guess. I have kidney disease and animal proteins are harder for my body to process. I look at my diet as medicine for my illness."

Hearing this, the mother-me immediately knocked the dude-me out of her chair and took over.

"Oh Hon, I'm sorry."

"It's okay. Just a shitty roll of the cosmic dice. Could be worse, I'm sure."

"So is there anything they can do? Will you get a transplant at some point?"

She rolled her napkin into a ball and stuffed it into the pocket of her belted jacket.

"Not really. For now I'm managing. The waiting list for an organ is years and years away but I wouldn't do it anyway."

"What? Why not?"

"I guess you could say I'm a Darwinist. Survival of the fittest and all that. I'm not a fan of western medicine and I'd rather just embrace my body, treat it well, and enjoy whatever life I have regardless of how long or short it might be."

I set down my water glass and leaned forward.

"I don't understand. You're a smart, insightful young woman with a bright future ahead of you. With so much to offer don't you feel a moral obligation to stick around as long as possible?"

"Ellie, I'm not willing to lead a half-life on dialysis. I'd rather live a full one up until the point my kidneys no longer function."

I couldn't believe what I was hearing and the healer in me wanted at her like duct tape on a busted lawn chair. Surely I could change her mind!

Before I had a chance to debate her last statement she stood and wrapped a red scarf around her long neck.

"You can keep the notes for now. I'm going for a walk."

"You sure?"

"Of course. I'll see you in class."

I watched Lucy empty her tray before striding though big double doors into the campus courtyard, long thin legs carrying her willowy body as if she were propelled by wings. A light rain started to fall and little droplets tapped at the cafeteria window as she drifted out of sight.

I shoved my plate aside and glanced down at her carefully written notes but my mind refused to release its grip on my heart. How could this lovely and intelligent young woman so easily detach from the likelihood of an untimely death? And what in the world could I do to convince her to change her mind? Of all the students in that class she was the one I'd noticed early on as she engaged the instructor in vigorous debates about everything from cultural brainwashing of young girls to the sexual slavery trade that operates right under our noses in this country.

Unable to study, I packed up my papers and headed toward the building that housed the humanities classes. Once serving as a National Guard facility, the scattered structures were gradually being modernized. No matter how ugly the building, one couldn't ignore the fact that the setting itself was fairly striking. Situated three miles north of San Luis Obispo, the campus is shadowed on the north side by Hollister Peak, one of nine volcanic cores leading to the Pacific Ocean, and across the street from a botanical garden. The former military compound has been transformed into an inviting web of walkways leading through trees with stunning views in most every direction.

Inside the classroom that afternoon I found myself watching Lucy as she huddled over the test questions. I no longer cared about my grade as much as I cared that this smart, ambitious young woman would probably die before me—thirty years her senior. It didn't seem fair that there weren't enough kidneys to go around. Perhaps the system for organ allocation needed to be fixed and she could be the poster child for change. She was already a fledgling activist; I could easily picture her leading marches and chants on Washington. The world needed more Lucy's, not less.

And in that moment it was as if a transformer blew up in the center of my being as Gandhi's famous words bubbled up to the surface: "Be the change you want to see in the world." Like a mantra, *be the change, be the change, be the change* played over and over in my head as I hurriedly filled in the rest of the little green circles on my scantron before practically throwing it on the instructor's desk.

I waited outside the classroom to catch Lucy before she got away. She was only a minute behind me and when she walked through the door I nearly attacked her.

"Lucy!"

"Oh hi, Ellie. Did my notes help?"

"Um, yeah, they were great. Here you go. Thanks for sharing them."

"You're welcome." She shoved the papers into her backpack. "Well, have a good one."

"Wait. Lucy, I've been thinking. I have two kidneys and I'd be happy to give you one."

She stared at me with intense green eyes, the kind that make you want to believe there really is such a thing as an old soul. They glistened just a little as she glanced downward then up again.

"Ellie that is really sweet of you to offer but they only let family members donate organs." She must have seen my heart sink to my feet as the words came out of her mouth. "And besides, I meant what I said. I don't want another kidney. I'm okay with this, really." She zipped up her backpack and flung it over her shoulder.

"But…"

Lucy took a step forward and rested her fine-boned hands on my shoulders.

"You can't save me because I don't need to be saved.

You're a really good person and I appreciate the huge offer you just made but please let it go." She took a step backward and smiled. "Okay?"

As I studied her face I recognized the steadfastness and resolve I'd seen on my own children's faces when I'd tried to change their minds.

"Okay," I said.

But I didn't really mean it.

TWO

March 2007

Spring in San Luis Obispo isn't so much a season as a sudden awareness of the jade-green hills that surround the *happiest place in America* turning the color of a lion's mane, while the buds on the trees burst into blossom seemingly overnight. For me, the apricot tree in my front yard is the gauge that measures the passage between these transitions. By the time the pinkish flowers turn to tiny bulbs of future fruit, the verdant hills have turned to a shade of lightly-browned toast and the next drop of rain won't fall until October.

It was sometime between this shift from green to brown that I learned I'd have to write a critical thinking paper as the final for English 101. The instructor, a curly-haired surfer who often taught class wearing shorts and sandals, offered a list of possible subjects, most of them having to do with environmentalism. The idea was to make an argument for change, then back it up with research. Although I've long been a dyed-in-the-dirt tree hugger, after weeks of perusing the list none of the suggested topics jumped out at me.

The instructor, who we called by his first name, Matt, said we could choose a topic of our own but that we'd have to submit a prospectus before moving forward with the final paper. I'd entertained arguing for carpool incentives on campus because the parking situation was becoming a real problem as more and more students drove rather than taking the bus—often without a passenger. I'd witnessed procrastination in my own son—also a student at Cuesta—on a daily basis since enrolling in college. If the administration offered students a prime parking spot closer to the classrooms they'd probably jump on the idea. It was a good topic and Matt immediately approved it but after a couple weeks of calling around to various college departments trying to find out whom I needed to talk to about offering incentives to carpoolers, I got nowhere and lost interest in the paper.

I hadn't seen Lucy since fall semester ended but she was still on my mind. It saddened me that she'd accepted her fate, partly due to a broken medical system that disallowed non-related donors. I'd given up trying to convince her to change her mind about an organ transplant but I hadn't forgotten about her. It suddenly occurred to me that the paper for my English final was an opportunity to argue for changing the rules about altruistic organ donation. I discarded the carpooling idea and started over.

My prospectus noted the tragic outcome due to many hospitals refusing to accept altruistic donors despite the lack of available organs. I wanted to challenge the ethics of these hospital rules, putting the onus on administrators for playing God by questioning the motivation of viable donors. Although he was disappointed I'd shelved the carpooling idea, Matt approved my topic and I immediately dove headfirst into the spidery world-wide web of fact and fiction with a newfound passion for a subject that was to become dear to my heart.

One of the websites I stumbled across in my research was kind of like a dating site for patients and potential organ donors called Matching Donors. I bookmarked the link and found myself returning to it several times to browse the heartbreaking pleas from people who hoped to find a donor for themselves or a loved one. I read through hundreds of poignant stories—mothers and fathers whose children needed an organ, loving wives and husbands, children and young adults who had been sick all their young lives. But the saddest profiles were the older patients. Reading their words you could sense their desperation. It reminded me of my visits to the animal shelter where day in and day out senior dogs and cats are passed over for perky puppies and happy-go-lucky kittens (with lots of life left in them), and so many of the white-whiskered animals are euthanized.

As I scrolled through the profiles I found myself creating a "what if?" scenario in my head, even going so far as to plug in my own blood type to discover potential recipients. *What if one of these patients lived nearby? What if I could find a transplant center that accepted non-related donors? What if I turned my words into action?* And *What if this hospice nurse in Northern California—a mother and new grandmother— what if we were a compatible match?* We both had the same blood type. We were close in age. From what I could read between the lines we likely even shared the same political leanings.

They say you can look back upon a person's life and you're likely to find one or two significant events that have impacted that person in ways that leaves him or her forever altered by the experience. These benchmarks of change might be a divorce, a death, a move, an addiction, a recovery, or some other momentous occurrence. Each passage leaves a noticeable mark on the individual—an existential metamorphosis of sorts. One rarely recognizes these permutations except in retrospect but when I read and reread this woman's bio that day something stirred inside me. I felt a visceral shift from curiosity to conviction as my hand hovered over the mouse.

To: Confidential Patient
Subject: More info requested
Hi:
I'm contemplating donating one of my kidneys. Tell me more about this process and what I need to know before

taking the next step. My heart aches for you after reading about your ordeal. Hang in there.
    Ellie

As you might imagine, this act, this one click of the *submit* button changed my life in ways unforeseeable at the time. From that moment forward I went from being a casual community college student writing a paper for a class to a woman on a mission to make a difference in someone's life. Someone I didn't (yet) know.
    Someone named Kathy.

To: Confidential Donor
Subject: RE: More info requested
Hello and thank you for your interest in helping me. To donate directly to me you would start by either knowing your blood type or you can have your blood checked for typing. My insurance covers all of your medical costs. The transplant center I work with is California Pacific in San Francisco; they would want to talk directly to you before we got started. They'll ask some basic health questions like if you have high blood pressure, any history of kidney problems, etc.
    My blood type is B+ and is fairly rare. Once you are cleared for type match then you would have some lab work done to be sure your health would not be compromised. California Pacific would send you the blood tubes etc. and you could have them drawn at your local lab/doctor's office and they would mail them to California Pacific. You would be informed of these test results even if you ended not being able to donate. The transplant would be done at California Pacific. Just so you know, this is a process that takes some time.
    Kathy

As I read Kathy's email it became clear that the proverbial

ball had rolled from my court into hers and volleyed back again. Except this was no game. This was someone's life with much more at stake than mild curiosity. From that moment on I was on her team, rooting for her to win the big trophy, or, more specifically, a healthy kidney.

I took a deep breath and hit *reply*.

Through a flurry of emails that followed I learned that Kathy and her husband Jim resided in a rural area near Arcata, California where they raised chickens and grew their own vegetables. Kathy and her two brothers all suffered from polycystic kidney disease, a hereditary condition causing masses to develop that debilitate renal function as it progresses. Her only daughter inherited PKD and had recently given birth to Kathy's first grandson. Jim and Kathy lived in a comfortable mobile home on property where they'd been building their dream house little by little over the past decade until Kathy's illness had put the project on hold. It was in that trailer that they'd been performing home dialysis three to four hours at a time, four to five nights a week.

What Kathy learned from me was that her prospective donor was a 48 year-old massage therapist with two grown daughters and six grandchildren in Michigan, and a son who lived at home. I told her how I'd met Lucy and written a paper about hospital policies that prevented altruistic donors from providing more options to patients and how the resulting lack of organs had spurred me to become involved. I assured her that I was healthy and excited about the prospect of donating.

Kathy requested I make sure donating was okay with my family before we proceeded, so the next afternoon I dialed up my oldest daughter Andrea and told her what I was planning to do.

She was silent for a moment and then said, "Mom, I have no doubt that if you give one of your kidneys to someone, one will be available to any of us should we ever have the need. That's just the way the world works."

Andrea and I might be separated by geography and religion (she's a conservative Christian and I'm a devout agnostic) but we share similar belief systems when it comes down to common humanity. She promised to talk with her sister Maggie and I told her I'd have a chat with her younger brother Jacob. He turned out to be a little tougher to convince than his oldest sibling.

I stopped my son on the way from a shower back to his bedroom. No matter how many times I'd begged him to towel dry his shaggy head of curls before he left the bathroom he'd still come out dripping. It was all I could do to focus on the subject matter instead of the water puddling on the new wood floor at his feet. I'd already shared my English paper with him so he was aware of my interest in organ donation but I hadn't yet told him I'd decided to become a donor. Jacob, as it turns out, wasn't concerned about himself or one of his sisters needing a kidney; he had doubts about my mental condition.

"Mom, you need to keep that shit. There's a reason you have two. In case one gets borked, you have a back-up."

"Lots of people are born with one kidney, Jacob, and they don't even know it. Our kidneys function at seven times the level we need. Seven-hundred percent!"

He looked at me seemingly unfazed by statistics gleaned from my research paper.

"You're still reducing that function by half. Why would you want to do that?"

"Because I believe I'll be just fine with one kidney and it'll help someone who really needs it."

He didn't exactly roll his eyes but he sighed a little.

"I get it. I don't necessarily agree with it but I'll support you if that's what you really want to do."

I smiled and told him that's all I wanted from him.

"Well I still hope you come to your senses and change your mind but yeah, I'm cool with it."

He turned and walked away, leaving a trail of wet

footprints in his wake.

***

Over the course of the next couple of weeks I gathered more information, more statistics, and more horrific patient outcomes than I'd ever expected. It became painfully clear how badly the system needed to be changed, starting with transplant hospitals that refused viable donors simply because they weren't known to the patient. Their reasoning was that it was unlikely an unrelated donor wouldn't have a hidden agenda, would be mentally stable, or have been pressured into donating. A person who chose to offer an organ to a fellow human being simply because they wanted to help was seemingly unimaginable to the overseers of transplant policy. In other words, a person like me.

THREE

April/May 2007

I sat in a wicker chair in the front yard and dialed Kathy's number, waiting through several rings before she picked up.

"Hello?"

"Hi. It's Ellie."

"It's so good of you to call. I don't know why but I wanted to hear your voice. I thought it'd be good if we talked on the phone instead of just exchanging emails."

"I agree," I said. In the background a hum, like a dishwasher running, distracted me from my train of thought. I hoped it would cycle off soon so I could hear her better. "How are you feeling?"

"I'm doing pretty well. We're almost an hour and a half in and this is where I start getting chilly. Jim's getting me a blanket. One sec." I heard a male's soft voice before Kathy came back on the line. "Jim says to say 'hi' and thank you."

It dawned on me then that the hum was their home dialysis unit. I pictured Kathy in an overstuffed chair with a stack of books nearby to occupy her as they waited for the machine to cleanse her blood. My imagined visuals were interrupted by a faint memory from childhood, a song we used to sing in church, and the refrain that went:

There is pow'r, pow'r, wonder-working pow'r
In the precious blood of the Lamb...

As a child I didn't understand the lyrics but the irony of

my prospective sacrifice juxtaposed against my agnosticism was suddenly overpowering. I could almost feel my deceased father's hand on my shoulder as I cupped the phone to my ear. It took every ounce of my attention on Kathy to remain composed.

"Is it painful?" I asked.

"The dialysis?"

"Yes. Does it hurt?"

"The needle for the catheter stings a bit but not the dialysis itself. Sometimes I get cold and a little weak if my blood pressure drops too suddenly. But I've been doing it for so long it's just part of life."

"How long?"

"About five years. We've only been able to do it at home for the last seven or eight months. We used to have to drive almost an hour each way to the renal center. Because we're so rural having the home option has been a real advantage for us. It's a lot of work but worth it not to have to travel."

Her voice sounded matter of fact, tired but even. It was difficult for me to imagine how they'd normalized spending most of their "free" time devoted to dialysis while both maintained full time jobs. I get antsy waiting in line for coffee. I can't imagine having to sit for four to five hours, unable to move from my chair at will, day after day, week after week, year after year.

"I wanted to let you know I talked with my children and they're on board with this," I said.

"I'm glad you spoke with them, Ellie. I think it's important to include family in such a serious decision. I have to tell you my coworkers are astounded by the fact that a complete stranger would be willing to donate her kidney. I don't think anyone, including Jim and I, ever really expected someone to come forward who didn't know us personally."

I tugged at a loose thread of wicker on the arm of the chair that our cats regularly used for a scratching post as I took in her words.

"Is that why you cancelled your Matching Donors profile?"

"Our subscription expired and we decided not to renew it. For now we'll just see what happens with you and me."

Throughout our conversation I'd watched a steady parade of dog-walkers, skateboarders, joggers, cyclists, and stroller-pushing parents pass in front of the house, having no idea how lucky they were not to be tied to a dialysis machine. I was lost in this thought when Kathy's voice brought me back.

"Jim needs to take my blood pressure, Ellie. Thanks so much for your call, and most especially for your generous offer. It's been good to talk with you."

"You too, Kathy. Let's just hope our blood samples do a happy dance in the lab together. I'll contact the local coordinator as soon as possible."

"Keep in mind these things take time. I've learned to be patient."

"Okay," I said, but I knew myself better. Waiting for those blood tests to come back would be a couple of the longest weeks of my life.

After we hung up I got down on my hands and knees to weed the front yard. I immediately punctured my skin on a baby century plant, possibly because I had murdered its mother the previous summer. One day the overgrown succulent growing along the edge of my front yard had thrown up a spike from the center of its massive and dangerously pointed leaves. I had thought it was about to flower, but as the days passed the huge asparagus-like protrusion continued to pierce the air, eventually surpassing the height of the nearest trees. The bigger it grew the more obscene it looked, especially mid-day when the top wilted to one side in the heat. I would feel myself flush when a car slowed down as I watered the lawn, as if I were purposely flaunting the vulgar plant that bordered my neighbor's yard.

When it kept growing for almost a month I searched the

Internet to find out just what kind of plant suddenly sprouts a thirty-foot phallus after sitting quietly for the previous six summers. Turned out it was a relative of the century plant which only blossoms every twenty-five years and then dies. I should have been sad to discover its pending fate, but I wasn't, really. I'd lost count of how many times those needle-tipped leaves had poked me in the arms, legs, and ass while I worked in the yard. Besides, at least a dozen small clones grew around the Big Kahuna just waiting to take its place.

And yet I couldn't seem to take my eyes off it. Not just because of its prodigious size but because the idea of something so magnificent throwing a party for itself before it died made me uncomfortable. This plant had squatted there on the bank all this time just waiting to spend itself on one big showy display, then *poof.* Done. Kaput. Normally I wouldn't have been so obsessed by a silly plant except that it made me question my own purpose. *What would be my parting flower?*

There comes a time in your life when you realize happiness cannot be measured by the hours of sunshine in a day, fat bank accounts, shiny cars in the driveway, or one's peg on the career ladder, but by the weight of each moment as it leaves you once and for all. There will always be another car, another day to prove yourself in the corporate world, another paycheck to deposit, but once a moment is squandered, there's no getting it back. I sometimes feel a quickening, like an invisible seam suddenly taken in, with each careless step across this finite life.

Something happens when you turn the bend toward fifty. Suddenly you feel the evaporation of life's numbered experiences and you begin to wonder if you've made the best of them. Did I infect others with a smile? Did I pause to notice the texture of wet grass under my feet? Did I give thanks for the unconditional love of these amazing creatures in my care? Will I remember how good this feels, the soft pillow under my head as I fall asleep tonight? You wonder if you've done enough, if you've tasted every bite, and given back at least as much as you've taken. And you even start to appreciate the delicate spine of a succulent leaf as it reaches for your tender skin on a long-shadowed afternoon.

***

A few days after speaking with Kathy, I received a call from Betsy, the local coordinator for California Pacific Medical Center (CPMC). She ran me through a telephone interview consisting of questions to determine that a) I was a physically healthy candidate, b) I wasn't a criminal, and c) I wasn't bat-shit crazy. Apparently wanting to donate a body part raises suspicions on the cuckoo-meter. Fortunately, I passed the preliminary screening and Betsy promised that the hospital transplant team would schedule a blood draw to be done on the same day Kathy was drawn so they could test them together for compatibility.

When the kit arrived, I marveled at the perfect row of little vials and one big vial along with a packet of labels and instructions for express shipment back to San Francisco. On our scheduled morning draws, I carefully packed the box into the handlebar basket of my vintage yellow bicycle and rode to the local lab, less than a mile from my house. When I approached the counter I was met with my first bureaucratic hurdle.

"Insurance?"

"I don't have any. The recipient's insurance pays for the lab work." I pointed at the papers inside the kit. "The letter of guaranteed payment is on top."

She frowned.

"Recipient?"

"Yes. I'm donating a kidney."

The woman punched a number into her phone, turning away from me as she quietly spoke into the receiver. As soon as she hung up she handed the kit back to me.

"We don't do these."

"What? Why not? I have to have it done today!"

I stood there, shocked, as she called out the next name on the waiting list. An elderly man wearing a plaid shirt tucked into too-short pants rose from his chair and stepped slowly past me toward the phlebotomy rooms.

"I'm sorry," said the woman in the white lab coat. "We don't accept third-party billing."

Tears stung at my eyes as she walked down the hall ahead of the old man. I had promised to do this and I was going to let everyone down, most especially Kathy.

From a corner of the room a woman's voice interrupted my pity party.

"Try Sierra Vista Hospital. They have a walk-in lab."

I looked around the room toward the voice, which had come from where a woman quietly leafed through a magazine.

"They do?"

She glanced up from her reading.

"It's open until noon."

"Thank you!" I said. I rushed out the door and jumped back on my bike with my precious cargo.

Ten minutes later I arrived at the second lab and although at first was met with the same apprehension, the receptionist made a call to CPMC, who verified the promise of payment. I filled out an intake form and waited my turn on a flowered loveseat as the clocked ticked away toward the latest possible Fed-Ex pick up to make it in time to San Francisco.

"Eldonna?"

A wispy young woman wearing designer-print scrubs called to me from the doorway and I followed her down the hall to a room with a one-armed plastic chair.

"Hi. My name's Annika. Left or right?"

"Left please," I said, because I had deep-tissue massages

to give in the afternoon and I'm fairly right-hand dominant.

Annika tapped at my inner elbow with her forefinger and smiled.

"You've got great veins."

"Why thank you," I said.

She verified my full name and date of birth before tying an inch-wide band of rubber around my upper arm.

"Make a fist," she said, then, "A little stick…"

I waited for the pinch but didn't feel a thing.

"Okay, you can relax your hand."

I uncurled my fist.

"You give great needle," I said. I felt grateful for the ease that followed a not-so-easy start to having my blood drawn.

Annika grinned.

"I try." She pulled the vial from the back end of the needle and replaced it with another, and then another. "I read your file," she said. "I think it's a really cool thing you're doing. Someone you know?"

"No. I mean yes. Well I *didn't* know her but now I do. We're getting to know each other."

She topped off the last vial and pulled the needle from my arm, covering the spot with a bandage and folding my hand upward in one swift motion.

"Keep it up there for a minute." Annika wrote my name and the date in tiny letters on each vial, checking and double-checking against the included list. "Okay, you're good to go."

"Do you think it will still make the FedEx pick-up?"

"I'll walk it over there myself," she said.

"Thank you, Annika."

"You're welcome. And good luck!"

***

Although I was at one time an excellent waitress, I am not so much an excellent wait-*er*. Preparation for final exams, parenting a teenager, working, and maintaining an older house kept my hands busy, but my brain kept circling back to *When will we know something? What are the odds we'll be a good match? What if the transplant center rejects me for not being related to the patient? How can we convince them to let us proceed?* And so on and so on, ad nauseam, until I thought my head would explode.

When two weeks had passed since the blood draw I made a call to Betsy to ask if she'd heard anything.

"The fact that we haven't any news yet is good news," she assured me. "It means you're probably a good type-match and they're waiting for the antigen test to see if Kathy's blood builds antibodies against yours, indicating likely organ rejection."

"How long does that take?"

"It varies, but two to four weeks is a normal time frame for results."

The longer we waited the more restless I became. I had an uneasy feeling we weren't going to be a good match, just like the other people who'd tested with Kathy before me. She'd warned me that due to having had blood transfusions her body had created an army of combatant antigens and that although she hoped we'd be a good match, her hopes were not all that high. So when we hadn't heard anything by the end of the second week I decided to go back to a few other profiles I'd saved on matchingdonors.com to see if they were still actively looking.

Sarah's * mother had posted a bio on her behalf, begging for help. Her daughter was in her thirties, otherwise healthy, a journalist living in Boston. They would pay for transportation if necessary. I decided it couldn't hurt to have a back-up plan. I wrote and told her that although I was being tested for another patient I was willing to also be tested for her daughter in case the first one didn't work out.

She called almost immediately.

"I'm in Florida but I'm giving you my daughter's number so you can contact her directly and take it from here. No matter what happens I just want to thank you for being an angel to someone." I could hear the desperation embedded in her east coast accent. She wanted to be happy for my other patient but, like any mother, was hoping against hope I would become her daughter's savior.

Sarah seemed genuinely surprised to hear from someone on the west coast. She sounded older than her age, which I assumed might be a result of fatigue and disease, but her voice mirrored her mother's cadence.

"My mother paid for that ad. She's a little more aggressive than I am. But thank you for contacting us. Are you sure the travel wouldn't be a problem?"

"I think it would be fine. I've read up on your hospital and they have a great recovery facility for donors."

"Well, if we match you'd only have to come here for the surgery. All the pre-testing can take place in your vicinity. Is there anything you want to know about me or the procedure?"

"I do have one question. I'm a little overwhelmed by reading these profiles and I'm wondering if I'm the only person who's contacted you so far."

"Actually, no. There was this man from Kansas, a mail-carrier, who not only was tested but turned out to be a good match. Unfortunately for me but very fortunately for him, they discovered he was in the early stages of kidney cancer when they did further pre-op tests."

"Seriously? What happened to him?"

"I was told he had the kidney removed and due to early detection he has a really good chance of a complete recovery."

"So in other words, had he not offered to donate he might not have known…"

"Until it was too late, yeah. Weird, isn't it? How things happen that way?"

"Talk about instant karma!"

"I know. We're still in touch. He felt really bad he couldn't donate and I was like, are you kidding me? It stuns me that people are so good, that they want to help just for the sake of helping." I was still taking the story in when she added, "And that's why my mother wanted to be in control of the ad. I think she assumes people have ulterior motives and might try to take advantage of us."

"I have no horse in this race, Sarah. You can assure your mother of that. I just want to help someone if I can."

"I know. I can tell just by talking with you. Thank you, Ellie."

"You're welcome. Have your transplant center contact me and we'll coordinate the blood tests. You do know I'm being tested for another patient, right?"

"I understand that. I appreciate your willingness to put me in a back-up position."

"Okay then. Good luck to us, Sarah."

"Bye, Ellie."

***

They say that news comes in threes. The first round in late May brought me all A's in the three classes I was taking at Cuesta College, which I had worked my butt off to achieve. The second was a call from Betsy to tell me that Kathy and I were not compatible due to antigen issues, however, CPMC had instituted a new "paired match" enterprise. In other words, they could input our information into a patient-sharing program and try to find another incompatible pair so that we could possibly swap donors with two others in our situation. Finally, I heard from Sarah's transplant team informing me that I was indeed a good match and asking if I was interested in scheduling pre-op tests.

I was beyond pleased that I'd managed to pull off a 4.0 when my brain was having a much harder time recalling information as I approached the fifty-year mark. But the second two pieces of news left me feeling conflicted. It reminded me of King Solomon having to determine which mother would get the baby whom both claimed was rightfully theirs. I had started out on this path just wanting to do some good in the world and now I'd put myself in the position of helping one at the possible expense of another.

As I pondered my dilemma, Sarah's mother called to ask if I'd heard the news.

"We had three possible donors tested and although all were good matches, we like you the best!"

"Three?"

"Yes, but I'm not sure I trust those other two. One of them has been in prison. I hired a private investigator. He's probably done drugs."

"Oh. Well I'm pretty sure the hosptial wouldn't accept anyone who didn't have a healthy kidney. How long ago was he incarcerated?"

"It was a long time ago and he's supposedly turned his life around but I still have concerns."

I explained to her that I'd been asked to consider the paired match program with Kathy here in California. Because she was so difficult to match, her chances would improve if she were attached to a viable donor. I told Sarah's mom that I needed to think about it before making a decision.

"Ellie, you do what you need to do. I understand. Again, thank you for considering my daughter."

"You're welcome. I'll be in touch in a few days, okay?"

I hung up the phone feeling completely torn. I knew how desperate I would be if it were one of my children. Yet having lost my mother before she got to see her grandchildren grow up, my heart ached for Kathy and her daughter.

So I did what I always do when I need to be alone with my thoughts. I filled the old claw foot bathtub that sits under a tree in my back yard. I let myself sink into the water, steam rising to meet the dark green leaves of our overgrown plum tree, my mind competing with my heart for the answer to a seemingly unanswerable question.

FOUR

June 2007

I've been a single mother on and off for most of my adult life. I tried hard to succeed at marriage(s), I really did, but I just wasn't very good at it. Or maybe I was too good at it in an over-reaching kind of way that ended with me feeling depleted and my partner scratching his head, looking at me like a car that suddenly stopped running for no reason. I had my reasons, plenty of them, reasons that could usually be distilled down to one simple caveat: an engine won't run on an empty tank. It wasn't my exes' fault really, because who can blame them for expecting me to keep giving when that was what they were used to?

It took a lot of years to finally understand the need for balance. That *no* is a complete sentence. That it's okay not to over-schedule massage clients when I'm tired or have other things to do. But there's an exception to every rule and for me, that exception stood in the form of my son, for whom I would have done almost anything to assure his happiness and success. That June, as I pondered what to do about my predicament with Kathy and Sarah, there was plenty to keep my mind busy. Namely Jacob.

People often noted that we were more like an old couple than mother and son the way we bickered and made up, shared a million inside jokes, fought over what went into the grocery cart. I suppose it's because he's the only male that's stuck around in my life for more than a few years—granted, more by necessity than choice. Or maybe it's due to the fact that from the instant I first laid eyes on this kid I understood he was as much my peer as my progeny.

As a child Jacob was the kind of kid who would sit cross-legged in the middle of the basketball court during summer camp, his spectacled head absorbed in a book while the other children danced the ball around and over him. He was the student consistently sent to the principal's office for distracting the class with his jokes, arguing semantics with a teacher, or standing up to a bully with words that sliced as deeply as the punches landing on my son. And he's the kind of kid you pull out of school a half-dozen times, trying unsuccessfully to find an odd-shaped hole for a many-faceted peg.

My son will be the first to admit he was not an easy kid to raise. I moved him from school to school, attempting to find a good fit, including home-schooling, a charter school, a boarding school, and, finally, a combination that allowed him to take classes at community college during his senior year of high school. He was also the reason I chose to take classes at Cuesta. I figured if I was driving him there anyway I might as well stick around and learn something. I suppose in retrospect he is partially the reason I ended up as a kidney donor. If I hadn't taken that class I wouldn't have met Lucy. If I hadn't met Lucy I probably wouldn't have chosen altruistic organ donation as my topic for an English paper. And if I hadn't had to research that paper I never would have read Kathy's profile.

For his high school graduation I gifted Jacob with Lasik surgery to correct his severe near-sightedness. I cannot begin to describe what a joy it was to watch him walk out of the surgery center seeing the world for the first time since second grade without glasses. Not only did it improve his eyesight, my son suddenly walked a little taller and his self-confidence increased. Girls began to make comments about his beautiful eyes, eyes that had been hidden behind thick lenses—often with broken frames—for most of his eighteen years.

His graduation ceremony was simple, sweet, and unrehearsed. The thirteen black-capped students each chose a song to accompany their walk to the stage, a semi-circle of chairs on the lawn. Jacob chose ELO's *Mr. Blue Sky*, fitting, in that it was his first public appearance sans prescription lens.

I know my kid loves me but he's not always been quick to say so. His way of showing affection was to crack my back when he noticed I was "off" or to pick up an extra pack of my favorite sunflower seeds when he was at the store. So I didn't expect much more than a posed photo or an indulgent hug on graduation day. What I got was a fitting reward for twelve-plus long years of trying to give Jacob the best education available.

He walked up to the front of our small gathering of other square pegs and their proud parents, tapped the mic, and said, "Wait. I thought I was the juggling act. No?"

Nervous laughs erupted from the faculty before he retrieved a folded sheet of paper from beneath his crooked cap and began to read.

The transition from high school onward never seemed like such a big deal to me. What's all the fuss about? After all, our schooling isn't complete, in fact far from it. If you were to ask me, or be forced to listen to me ramble on as you all are, I would say that our schooling ends with a toe tag. There are so many things to discover and explore on this planet—from new sources of renewable energy to unseen species of tropical insects to new planets and stars not yet seen or given a name. Whether we go on to college or find what we love in a simpler life, whether we travel abroad or deeply explore the comforts of home, we will spend the rest of our lives learning the complicated rhythms of the Earth.

So what are we really graduating from? I sat at my

computer for hours, unable to write more than a sentence about my graduation (then again, the James Bond marathon on TV didn't help). I was stumped. Finally, it dawned on me. I think graduation isn't just a celebration of what we've done—although anyone who has sat through public school lessons that made eating glass look more appealing (and most of us have) deserves a medal. No, nearly everyone has endured twelve years of standardized, platform-building schooling that in and of itself is good mostly for celebration that it's finally over.

The real focus of graduation, however, is the glorious recognition and anticipation of all the varied and amazing things we will do in our lifetimes, the things that we'll learn from here on out—be it thermonuclear physics, computer science, art, or underwater basket weaving. Raising a family, caring for loved ones, discovering the balance of work and play; from this day forward we each break free of standardized credit mongering and walk our own paths in life, building the tools that you—not the State of California— decide you need, and discovering what it is in life that makes your heart sing.

Ralph Waldo Emerson once said, "To be yourself in a world that is constantly trying to make you something else is the greatest accomplishment." Then again, he also said that quotation confesses inferiority, so maybe he wasn't the best guy to quote.

In closing, no graduation speech would be anywhere near complete without the standard thank you to a very unstandard woman. I spent what often seemed like every day of first through eighth grade getting my cheeky butt sent to the office, so my mother got to know a lot of secretaries very well. If it weren't for my mother's tireless work, I would never have received such a varied and exceptional education.

Words can't begin to describe how thankful I am for your constant support and guidance, and the support and guidance I will no doubt require when I need to figure out *how to do my taxes, or buy a house, or make pot roast, or take bubblegum out of my couch. If anyone deserves a cool little piece of paper and a nifty hat, it's totally you, mom. If Mr. Emerson will allow me to quote him yet again, even if it does confess my inferiority, "Men are what their mothers make them."*

At this point he ad-libbed, "And now if you'll all indulge me, I've got some flowers here for my mom and for my teacher Amy, who put up with a long year's worth of procrastination and nincompoopery from me." He produced a beautiful bunch of roses for me and a bouquet of mixed flowers for Amy, handing them to us one at a time. There wasn't a dry eye on the lawn.

I share this story because when people heard that I wanted to donate a kidney they had a difficult time understanding why I would do such a thing. I told them for the same reason I spent a couple years paying off Lasik surgery on a massage therapist's income: because giving someone a healthier, happier way to be in the world is one of the best gifts you can give, one that gives back to you a sense of well-being and purpose beyond explanation. There were times when I thought all my hard work went unappreciated by my son but I was wrong. Sometimes you just have to trust that what you put out into the world will, at some point, blow back a blessing. Sometimes it's immediate, sometimes it takes eighteen years.

People often ask, "Well it's one thing to do something for your family, but a stranger?"

And this is where it's difficult not to sound hokey, but truly, I believe we are all, in a sense, family. I believe actions have a ripple effect and when you put goodness out into the world it creates a wave that spreads beyond the realm of our perception. The people on the organ waiting lists have mothers and fathers, siblings, partners, friends, and co-workers who are equally affected by the result of their friend or loved one receiving an organ. I might not be able to see it as clearly as I saw the effect "new eyes" had on my son, but when I made the decision to donate I trusted the impact would be even greater, given that wearing glasses is a heck of a lot easier than kidney dialysis.

On the Monday after my son's graduation ceremony I called the transplant coordinator and asked her to sign me up for the Paired Exchange program with Kathy. My reasoning was that Sarah had other donors while Kathy did not. Also, Kathy's transplant center was only a few hours from me, meaning my surgery would be less complicated by long-distance travel. Finally, I liked the idea of being able to help facilitate two patients getting a kidney rather than just one. The benefit from a paired exchange had the potential to create a tidal wave of grace that would reach beyond the limits of my imaginings. How could I resist?

Kathy called the following week to thank me.

"I'm trying not to get my hopes up," she said. "I know I'm difficult to match."

"Well it can't hurt to try, right?"

"I can't thank you enough, Ellie."

"No problem. I would have always wondered if I'd walked away before the last hand was played."

"You're the one taking the gamble, not me," she said.

The truth is, every day of her life was a gamble. Between veins closing and heart problems or blood pressure issues associated with PKD, Kathy never knew how long she would have with her husband, her daughter, or her new grandson. I, on the other hand, would go about my happy life in reasonably good health and live a statistically long life, regardless of whether or not we found a matched pair.

"Have fun with your family this weekend, Kathy. Say hi to Jim for me."

I leaned down and stroked Bella, who'd patiently waited at my feet for her overdue walk while I'd been on the phone. At six years old she was still somewhat of a puppy although a few gray hairs had started to sprout under her chin. She's part lab and part everything-else-on-the-block, with the most soulful brown eyes I've ever had the joy of peering into. I'd always been more of a cat person, as evidenced by the two felines snoring at the end of my bed, but this girl and I share a bond that cemented on the day we first met.

It was already hot that June morning six years earlier when I'd driven a few miles south of town to a flea market to scout for used books. As I passed a vendor selling leather-tooled belts I noticed a little black puppy panting in the bed of his rusty truck.

"He looks thirsty," I said.

The man glanced at the dog and shrugged.

"Can I give him a little water?"

The owner groaned as he rose from his lawn chair and scooped up the floppy-eared pup.

"*Her*," he said, handing me the dog. "Last one of the litter."

I poured water from a bottle into my cupped hands and the puppy lapped up every last drop. I filled them two more times before she'd had enough. When I rubbed her velvet ears between my fingers she wagged her tail but she was trembling.

"She's so cute. What's her breed?"

"Mother's a black lab. Father's a Border Collie, we think."

A bearded man strolled up and started browsing the man's wares.

"Okay if I take her for a little walk?" I asked.

The vendor grabbed a piece of frayed clothesline from the back of his truck and handed it to me.

"Suit yourself," he said, and turned back to his customer.

The puppy would walk a few steps then stop, walk a few steps, then stop. I didn't know if she was too hot or just afraid of all the people tramping by so I picked her up and carried her around as I strolled down a couple of rows.

Several people stopped to pet her and remark about what a cute puppy I owned.

"She's not mine," I'd say. "I'm just taking her out for a bit."

After about twenty minutes of paying more attention to the fur-ball in my arms than any of the items for sale, I headed back down the row toward the belt guy. Except that it was the wrong row apparently, so I traveled back up the next one and the one after that before coming back to the first row again. Eventually I found the space, a broken buckle on the ground where the man's table had been less than half an hour earlier.

I moved to the adjacent booth where a near-toothless woman was selling used clothing. Her young daughter sat on a blanket folding and stacking vintage jeans. The girl looked just like her mom except that she was only missing her two front teeth.

"Excuse me," I said. "Do you know when the man who was next to you is coming back?"

She looked at the pup in my arms and shot me a gummy grin.

"I believe he left about half an hour ago. Said he got rid of what he was most hoping to unload."

"But I was just taking her for a walk!"

A teenage couple ambled up and the girl squealed with delight as she begged to hold the puppy.

"He's so beautiful!"

"*Her*!" I said, as I handed the girl the sleepy dog. "But she's not—"

The older woman couldn't help herself. She laughed a big wheezy smoker's laugh that as creepy as it was, made me laugh, too.

"What's her name?"

I took the puppy back and held her face just a few inches away from mine.

"Bella," I said, still laughing. "Her name is Bella."

By the time I brought her home I'd already stopped for dog food, a collar, and a leash. By the time she curled up next to Jacob while two very pissed-off cats watched from the other side of the room, we'd both fallen in love. And by the time Jacob took her with him to boarding school a couple years later I missed her so much I went out and got a spotted dog named Moxie. I adored the new girl but she never embedded herself in my heart like Bella. When Jacob went off to UCSC several years later, he took Moxie and I kept Bella.

As I type these words Bella is on the floor at my feet, snoring. She's developed several benign tumors, the largest of which looks like a big hairy plum hanging from her back left knee. Her muzzle is almost completely white and she farts constantly but still looks at me the same way she did when I took her off that truck. If there were ever a reason to believe in the possibility of a perfectly paired match, she's it.

FIVE

July/August 2007

June came and went with no news from the transplant center about a paired match for Kathy and me. I still hadn't told many people what I was doing because everything seemed so up-in-the-air in terms of the how and when of the donation. I could say I tried to keep busy but I didn't have to try. Between painting the house, adding a room onto the back, and having my six year-old grandson for a month long visit, the summer flew by.

Jacob and I lived in a small two-bedroom bungalow on the northwest side of town that I'd bought shortly after my divorce in 2001. California real estate doesn't come cheaply. My son and I lived in a studio apartment for six months while I scoured the want-ads for a possible home. As a single self-employed parent this would be no easy feat. The most I could hope for was a mobile home and the least was to rent or move somewhere more affordable. But after living in SLO (as we locals call it) for five years, it had become my home, *our* home, and I was determined to stay put.

While perusing the ads in a local coffee shop one afternoon in the winter of 2000, a couple at the next table asked if they could borrow my newspaper when I was through. They were looking for investment property at a time when prices had fallen and had noticed me scanning the real estate section. Following a brief conversation, they scooted their table next to mine and we became housing cohorts, circling and underlining prospective open houses and for-sale-by-owners together. Having been a Realtor in Michigan before becoming a massage therapist, I was able to offer advice on what to look for in a good investment. Having honed in on the local market for several months, the couple shared inside information on houses not listed in the paper.

"There's a fixer-upper a block off Highland with a lease option," the wife told me. "We looked at it because it's close enough to Cal Poly's campus that it'd probably be a good rental yet still in a nice residential neighborhood."

"Why didn't you buy it?"

"Since then we've decided to look further south."

Her husband pulled a scrap of paper from his wallet and handed it to me.

"Here's the owner's number. Give him a call."

Husband and wife exchanged a knowing glance, the kind of surreptitious communication you develop over years of sharing secrets and arguments and love.

"What?" I asked.

They looked at each other again.

"Tell her," he said, nudging his partner.

"Well the owner is a bit...*difficult*. Be careful. But the terms would be perfect for someone in your situation. It'd give you five years to get on your feet, build sweat equity, and establish your credit."

I'd dealt with my share of difficult buyers and sellers. I figured I could handle one more cranky homeowner, especially if it meant getting us into a house in SLO.

But that was before I'd met Howie*.

When I pulled up to the house I didn't see him right away. This was because the top half of his body was tipped into the back of his trunk, taking a swig of whiskey and capping the bottle before bumping his head on the lid.

"Goddamnit! Sonofabitch!"

I stood in the driveway and waited for him to collect

himself before greeting him with a handshake. Dead grass and weeds had taken over the front yard but it was a big lot and I could easily see it filled with beautiful plants and shrubs. Under the carport an old boat that belonged to one of his tenants sat on a trailer with a flat tire. Faded blue paint covered the exterior stucco walls, chipped and cracked in many places. *Paint is an easy fix*, I thought, as I ticked off improvements. The single-pane crank windows would be a much bigger investment to replace.

"Hi. I'm Ellie. We talked on the phone yesterday."

Howie stood several inches shorter than me, the skin on his face the texture of overcooked bacon. He looked me up and down as though sizing up a horse, holding onto my hand with his calloused one even after I started to take mine back.

"Come on in, Honey," he said, patting my upper arm. He reached across my back before I sidestepped away as we walked up the drive.

Once inside I was delighted to find original hardwood floors. I was not so delighted to discover that they were stained with what appeared to be animal urine in the center of the living room. We toured the rest of the house where stick-on mirrors had been adhered to the bedroom walls, the toilet was leaking, and old metal cabinets hung over dark green linoleum countertops. Holes punctuated the wall at the far end of the kitchen where Howie had been working on the plumbing. Someone had stenciled gaudy grapevines near the ceiling to try and cheer the room up but the result was neither cheery nor inviting.

I followed Howie to where the jungle theme from the kitchen border spilled into the back yard. A tangle of overgrown vines and trees that were originally intended to be manicured bushes dominated a grassless lot heaped with piles of rusting junk. Surrounding the yard, several sections of a dilapidated redwood fence leaned toward the ground like tired soldiers giving up at the end of a long battle. The costs of improvements spilled onto an imaginary second page and I wondered if I'd have enough money left over after the down payment to fix up this house.

Howie sneaked up behind me and whispered into my ear, his pungent breath reaching my nose before the words even formed.

"Let's go look at the granny unit, Sweetie."

I kept a couple steps ahead of him as we walked to the converted garage attached to the west side of the house. Howie knocked on the door but I doubted whoever was inside would hear us over the blaring TV. He knocked again, this time banging with his fist.

"It's Howie! Let me in, Goddamnit!"

The door cracked open and a bearded face with wild grey eyes under bushy brows appeared in the space between the door and the jamb.

"I'm busy," said the head.

Howie pushed his way inside and I followed, half expecting to see R-E-D-R-U-M written across the walls. There was no graffiti but plenty of paint: several colors on half-finished walls, mostly pumpkin orange over what used to be white but had turned a grayish-brown. In the corner of the room a dirty mattress piled with rumpled sheets and blankets rested on the floor. A TV, precariously balanced on a three-legged table that was shabby but definitely not chic, stood in the center of the room. It was the only piece of furniture.

Off to one end of the studio, an old O'Keefe and Merritt stove sat under a bare light bulb that hung from the ceiling in the kitchenette, the oven door slightly ajar. Grease coated the light fixture and much of the walls. The leaky back bedroom housed a stack of moldy lumber and an old bicycle that stood in a puddle of water. Between the dank smell, the noise coming from the television, and the two men arguing, my senses hit their saturation level. Overwhelmed, I practically ran out the front door. I'd almost made it to my car when Howie caught up with me.

"It needs a little TLC but it's a good house for someone like you, Honey."

I wondered how someone like me would even consider buying this hell-hole.

"You're asking $250k with twenty-five down, right?"

"Six percent interest with a five-year balloon. Take or leave it."

"I need to think about it," I said.

His mouth went from a smile to pursed lips.

"Screw you! You go to the bank and see if you can get those terms!" he spat. "Goddamn tire-kickers!"

And off he went to his mobile bar for another drink. The last I saw of Howie that day was two short legs sticking out of the trunk of his Lincoln as I headed back to the coffee shop to look through the newest real estate ads.

I found nothing. Nothing I could afford, anyway. Jacob and I would to have to continue renting a tiny studio or move somewhere more affordable and start over. Again.

I called Howie the next day.

"$265,000 less your down payment, seven percent interest and we've got a deal," he said.

"I thought we'd agreed on $250k and six percent interest?"

"We didn't agree on nothin' young lady. That's my terms, take 'em or leave 'em."

I took 'em, along with seventeen loads to the dump, thousands of dollars in repairs, and nearly a decade of years to turn that ramshackle pit into a warm and welcoming home. I rented out the house to a Cal Poly professor. After gutting it down to the studs and putting up new drywall to get rid of the stink, Jacob and I moved into the granny unit. My son slept in a loft over his toy box at one end of the living room and I took the back bedroom after reroofing, recarpeting, and rewiring it. When Jacob turned twelve a year later, we lugged our few belongings into the house next door and rented out the granny unit to a local waiter. I'd completely drained my savings but we had a livable home, our own bedrooms, food on the thrift-store table, and that was enough.

More than enough.

***

Home, for me, is much more than a set of walls, a roof, and a yard. Our urban oasis had become somewhat of a legend in its own right over the years. Part commune and part boarding house, when rooms became available new students vied for the privilege of living in the pink house that welcomed its various residents. Having had to share his house with various revolving residents, I'd worked hard to make our place still feel welcoming for my son. Every summer I tried to add one major improvement to our little homestead. It had taken six years to landscape the yard, replace the roof and switch out the old crank windows. This was the summer I'd decided to paint the house a cheerful pinkish color with bright blue trim over the fading baby-blue exterior.

When my neighbor to the west strolled up the driveway I felt my shoulders edge up just a bit closer to my ears in the way they do when I worry. I assumed she was coming over to tell me the "hood" had gotten together and decided I'd crossed the line this time. As if the front yard planted in wildflowers, a massage trailer in the driveway, and various student boarders weren't enough, now I'd gone and painted my house in colors that belonged in San Francisco or Mexico or some other godforsaken place where foreigners, queers, and free-spirited hippie types live.

I was wrong.

What she said when she reached me was, "I really like your colors. It looks like such a happy house."

My shoulders relaxed. I curled my toes into the powdery edge of the waist-high pile of dirt in the driveway and smiled.

"Really? You don't hate it? I bet Mr. B. hates it."

"No, he likes it too. In fact it's pretty close to the color he had in mind for painting our house next year. Not quite as pink, not quite as intense, but kind of that same salmon vibe you've got going."

"It's called *hair ribbon*," I said. "The trim and awnings are *pacific blue*."

"It's inviting. Like you'd expect to walk up and find a tiny bistro in the front yard."

She glanced at the dirt pile.

"Oh, don't worry, this will all disappear as soon as I finish wheel-barrowing it to the back yard. I'm getting ready to pour a patio bit by bit." I winked at her. "Kind of how Mr. B built your deck a little at a time so the, ahem, city wouldn't get too curious."

She grinned.

"You've put a lot of hard work into improvements."

"And most of my earnings. Sometimes I think I should just sell and buy a condo."

"We don't want you to move, Ellie. You're a good neighbor."

"Thanks," I said.

Mrs. B. wandered back toward her clean-cut beige house with a neatly-trimmed lawn and beveled glass door. When she reached the walkway she turned and nodded toward our Harley-riding neighbor across the street who hasn't painted his house in twenty years. The only saving grace is that his home is several shades of chipped and cracked green so it kind of fades into the mountain behind it.

"Don't ask him, by the way. He absolutely hates it," she said.

'Well we're even then. These colors still aren't nearly as loud as his motorcycle."

A black Jeep pulled up and dropped Jacob at the curb. He waved at our neighbor and stopped to pet Bella, who lay in the shade of our plum tree.

"My friend Nina says our house looks like an Andy Warhol painting," he said. Then noticing the shovel and the dirt pile, made a beeline for the house before I had a chance to ask for help.

As I filled the wheelbarrow I thought about how color is a reflection of one's emotions, how after a couple years of disappointments I'd finally begun to bloom again. Of all the places I'd lived no other home had witnessed so many changes in my life. Those walls had echoed the boisterous laughter of uncontained joy, absorbed wracking sobs of grief and loss, and mirrored the excited welcomes and the teary good-byes of friends. My house now reflected the happiness I'd created within myself, *by* myself, in the years since choosing to remain un-partnered. My own foundation felt stronger, my outlook, like the new replacement windows, clearer and brighter.

I rested my chin on the shovel handle, the blinding sun rising to mid-sky like a prom dress at the owner's momentous reveal. Wiping my brow, I stabbed the blade into the middle of the pile and headed inside for a cup of iced coffee. I'd fully intended to return to the task at hand but the shovel remained like a flagless pole in a pile of potential. Instead of moving dirt, I moved my fingers across the mouse pad until I'd found and ordered the final touch, a bistro table and chairs to complete the roaring, reckless smile on the face of my happy house.

***

Owning and maintaining an old house has taught me that things take time. This realization didn't make it any easier to deal with the fact that Kathy and I hadn't hit gold in our first computer search for a matching pair with compatible blood markers. Waiting for news from CPMC had stretched over the months without a word and I was starting to lose my optimism. I'd naively imagined that by the end of summer I'd be walking around with one less kidney, Kathy would be off dialysis, and her caretaker husband, Jim, would be feeling the relief as well. In a perfect textbook case, that's what would have happened. In our case, it did not.

Not only did I still have both kidneys over the summer I had an extra person, my six year-old grandson, for almost half of it. He was delivered to me via the belly of an American Airlines jet where Jacob and a friend picked him up at LAX. Jacob said CJ never stopped talking from the moment he got into the car until they pulled in my driveway four hours hence. And also that his feet never stopped stinking, having arrived bare feet in tennis shoes that were kicked off immediately, nearly asphyxiating both driver and passenger.

At forty-eight, I'd forgotten what it meant to parent a small child 24/7. And yet after making a greater and deeper acquaintance with this beautiful boy I could no longer contemplate what life would be like minus his presence without feeling my heart bend at the center. Over five short weeks I re-learned a lot about being a small boy, things you forget even when it's only been a dozen years since your youngest was his age. Like how fun it is to snuggle in the back of a station wagon at the drive-in theater with Grandma and Uncle Jacob. That falling asleep comes easier after Dr. Seuss and a back scratch. That a Spiderman t-shirt goes with everything and Power Ranger slippers serve as street shoes until you wear holes in the bottom. That spinach is yucky but catsup goes with everything. And that a six year-old boy will expend more energy in the first hour of his day than I have on reserve for most of the week.

I accomplished almost nothing during the weeks CJ stayed with us. Best intentions were interrupted by bursts of joyous enthusiasm and requests for assistance with things that people with longer legs and billfolds take for granted, like reaching for the box of candy on top of the cupboards or buying a sticker book filed with happy faces and zoo animals. We made trips to the library, got our faces painted at the farmer's market, found out one of us can't swim (halfway down the pool slide), and ate frozen yogurt by the quart. We baked brownies, drew bubble baths, rode go-karts, and occasionally played a video game or watched a movie with Uncle Jacob when Grandma was too pooped to keep her own rules.

On our last morning together CJ slept next to me with a Pooh blanket over his head and clutching the stuffed puppy I'd sent to greet him at the airport in my stead. Normally he'd have been awake by seven but we'd stayed up to howl at the full moon over the fence in the back yard the night before. I knew it wouldn't be but a few minutes before he'd untangle himself from super-hero dreams to begin humming, something he did every day, all day, often into the night. It drove me a bit cuckoo at times, that constant nonsensical sound made just for the sake of its own noise. And yet when I put him back on the plane for Michigan later that morning the lack of his voice felt like a missing limb.

Kathy called as I was wiping precious fingerprints from the lower half of the living room walls. The minute I heard her voice on the other end of the line I assumed it was good news.

It wasn't.

"The transplant center is uncomfortable with us not knowing each other. Their policy prohibits altruistic donors." She sounded tired.

"Well I *do* know you, in all the ways that matter."

"I feel the same way, Ellie. Jim and I were wondering if you might like to come up here for a visit. And maybe we'd come down and see you later this year."

"Aha! That way they can't say we don't know each other!"

"Well, that, and we'd genuinely love to have you as our guest. It's beautiful up here you know. Maybe you could use a break."

"I've just had a kindergartener for over a month. I could definitely use a little down time," I said.

"How about the end of this month?"

I drew a thick red line though the last week of September on my planner.

"That sounds just about perfect."

"Okay, well just let me know when you'll arrive and we'll plan on you."

"No word from the—"

"Nothing," she interrupted me. "Don't worry. It'll happen when it happens."

"Thanks for the invitation. I really would love to meet you and Jim in person."

"You're welcome. And thank you for hanging in there, Ellie."

I picked up a photograph I'd snapped of CJ outside the local yogurt shop. He sat on a bench with the words, "Spit, Bitch and Chew" burned into the backboards. In the photo my grandson grinned at me from beneath his baseball cap, his tongue stabbing at a chocolate cone, one shoe on, one shoe off. If there's one thing you learn from a six year-old, it's about living in the moment.

"Not a problem, Kathy. We'll just take it one day at a time."

SIX

Fall 2007

I found it a lot easier to take one day at a time if I kept myself busy. A few weeks before, Cal Poly had informed me that after a five year wait I'd finally moved to the top of the list of potential ushers at the Performing Arts Center. With the price of tickets being so high I'd signed up to volunteer at the PAC in exchange for getting to see shows I wouldn't normally be able to afford. I immediately responded that I was indeed still interested.

Orientation took place the first weekend in September, at which I was the youngest trainee among mostly-retired folks. In addition to learning the layout and ticketing procedures, the trainers told us to blend in as much as possible. No sparkly jewelry or earrings bigger than a quarter were allowed. We were required to wear sensible black shoes, stockings—even in summer—a black vest over a white oxford shirt and a black skirt or slacks.

Although my wardrobe predominantly favors flowing skirts, yoga pants, tank tops and flip flops in a rainbow of pastel colors, I figured wearing the uniform was a small price to pay in exchange for attending musicals and other live performances. However, I'd forgotten one important aspect of my physical presence: the pink-dyed hair at the nape of my neck. One would think that if ninety percent of the ushers sported blue hair, a few strands of pink wouldn't be a big deal. But after receiving a glaring stink-eye from the floor captain upon noticing my colorful tresses, I spent hours perfecting ways to tuck the fuchsia tips under a barrette in order to obscure my individuality in favor of anonymity. In the end it took a large flower to cover it all, which was definitely bigger than a quarter and probably more attention-getting than the hair itself, but seemed to satisfy the trainer at the next event.

Despite my perfected hair camouflage I was unable to conceal my natural way of interacting with people. Once again I was approached by one of the more seasoned ushers, who pulled me aside in the lobby. She was friendlier than the first woman but told me not to touch people.

"What do you mean? Like not shake their hand?"

"Not only that, you can't touch a patron at all. It's against policy."

"I see," I said. "I'll do my best."

The rest of the evening I found myself jerking my hand away every time I went to rest it on a shoulder as I welcomed a geriatric patron, or instinctively moved to ruffle a child's curls. I must have looked like a bandleader the way my hands convulsed in front of my body as I reacted against any natural urge to touch people. In the end I found it impossible and finally just gave up. I'm a paid toucher, after all. It's what I do. It's what I *am*. I was never reprimanded again so either they were short on ushers or just decided that my touching patrons was better than constantly appearing to be on the verge of a seizure.

A week before I was to visit Kathy and Jim I ushered a matinee performance of Charlotte's Web for local schoolchildren. Seen through adult eyes, the corny props and melodramatic acting was over the top but as I looked across the rows and rows of young faces, every single gaze was glued to the stage. Some laughed, some nudged their neighbor, and some watched between parted fingers in front of their faces during the scarier parts. I couldn't help but think about how quickly we lose that innocent capacity to suspend disbelief in favor of doubt and cynicism.

Watching the play, I gradually gained a new appreciation for E.B. White's ability not only to weave messages into a spider's web, but lace a tapestry of truths throughout a story that remains compelling to people of all ages. The underlying message about the circle of life and death is pretty heavy stuff for elementary students but told in a way that stresses the value of friendship and working together as a community. Being the kind of person who enjoys finding connections in everyday synchronicity, Charlotte's plea to save Wilbur from an untimely death reminded me of the appeals for help I'd read on the matching donors website.

When the children filed out from the play, squealing and laughing amongst themselves, I thought about Kathy's young grandson and how she must wonder if she'll be alive to witness these years with him, and him with her. It struck me how much I take for granted, including not wanting to usher this particular event in the first place because I'd hoped to see a more interesting show. I hadn't imagined that the best part wouldn't occur on the stage but within the sea of innocence watching from below.

***

My flight landed early, giving me time to retrieve my luggage—a faded black duffel with a bright pink bow tied to the handle. Kathy had promised to wear an orange scarf and I promised to wear a pink one, although it probably wouldn't be very difficult for her to spot the blond with fuchsia pigtails and I was right. We recognized each other immediately. The hug said quietly what we'd not yet said aloud; *I may not know you but I already love you.*

"I'm sorry," she said, as we found her car in the small airport parking lot, "but I have to make a hospice stop in McKinleyville."

"No worries. I've got a book I started on the plane."

When we arrived at the convalescent home in McKinleyville where Kathy sometimes works, she rolled her window down for a female aide who greeted her beside the car.

"It's time," the aide whispered.

Kathy nodded and followed her into the care center. As I waited in the front seat of Kathy's station wagon my mind traveled back to those days leading up to own my mother's passing. I knew the drill— the drip, drip, drip of morphine, my dad pacing, the cookies my sisters and I baked for the hospice team in unending gratitude for the grace they delivered. I could almost hear the wails that followed my mother's last breath, wails I imagine permanently etched into the walls of my parent's former home.

When Kathy returned she was quiet except to say that her patient would be gone by morning and she'd done her best to make him comfortable. We rode the rest of the way mostly in silence. Upon reaching her driveway, we waited for twin fawns to finish grazing before winding our way to the little trailer that sat in the middle of five mostly-wooded acres. Kathy let half a dozen chickens out of their coop and they scattered noisily toward a neighbor's field of cows before running back to the yard, cluck-clucking.

Shoulder to shoulder in her tiny kitchen that afternoon, Kathy and I chopped fresh vegetables from their garden and tossed them into a well-used wok. An hour later Jim pulled into the drive, chattering with the chickens on his way inside. A quiet, bespectacled man with a quick smile and easy gait, he kissed his wife and greeted me warmly before setting the table for our meal. Over dinner we talked about our children, their new grandchild—everything except our hopes for a paired donor, perhaps in fear of jinxing ourselves.

After dessert they set about prepping R2, their name for her home dialysis machine. As they laid out needles and plugged in tubes, Kathy and Jim took turns explaining everything to me as if this was what every normal family did after dinner. As if she weren't already bracing herself for two fat needles to find purchase in the arm she was in danger of losing due to repeated dialysis.

I had a million questions but did my best to narrow it down to just a few.

"What's with the little bean bag pillows?"

"We warm them in the microwave and lay them on top of the tube that goes into my arm. Think about how cold "room temperature" would feel if you took a bath in it. That's what it feels like when the blood goes back into my body if I'm not able to warm it first."

Jim used the handle of his scissors to tap the lines leading from the machine to the tube that would go into Kathy's arm.

"Getting the air bubbles out?"

"Exactly," he said, turning dials on the front of R2 and recording the date onto a whiteboard that hung in the dining room wall.

Kathy lowered herself into a green recliner, her long legs crossed at the ankles. She opened a small packet of Betadyne and swiped it across her left arm. I resisted the urge to look away as she plunged a needle into her vein. Jim was waiting with blue tape that he'd cut into several short lengths ahead of time and gently placed across the needle to hold it in place.

The dialysis machine churned away as Kathy and I chatted. When a timer went off, Jim pumped up the cuff on her right arm and Kathy used the stethoscope around her neck to check her pulse. After recording the numbers Jim slipped the cuff off her arm and draped a blanket across his wife's lap. He disappeared and returned with a bowl filled with colorful candies. Before I could ask he answered me.

"She needs to spike her blood sugar, which tends to drop during dialysis."

"Skittles for dessert," Kathy said, giggling.

As Jim ran a tube from the back of R2 to the sink he explained that this part was the equivalent of "peeing" for Kathy.

"So, let me see if I understand dialysis," I said. "Kathy's kidneys fail to take the waste out of her body so one tube moves her blood through the machine, removes the toxins, then pumps the blood back into her body. The tube running to the sink is the fluid containing those toxins?"

"Pretty much, yeah." Jim smiled. "You've done your homework."

"If looking it up on Wikipedia counts as homework, and I think my son would vouch that it does, I did read up a bit after deciding to donate."

Jim pulled another container of saline water from a box. "Looks like four bags tonight, dear," he said.

In between doting on his beloved wife, Jim charted times and dates and milligrams of this and that, checked the dials, and double-checked the tubes leading in and out of Kathy and the dialysis machine. It was beyond me how they managed to make what was surely a daunting task of tracking multitudes of information seem so organized and seamless. I have a hard time not burning toast.

The next morning Kathy showed me photos of Jim and her pouring the foundation, raising the walls, and nailing the roof before giving me a tour of the dream home she and Jim had been building for over a decade, mostly by themselves. Kathy had created each tile from clay, fired it, and set them one by one on the bathroom floor. Over the past year she'd been building the front steps one stone at a time and encouraged me to place one, but I didn't want to mess up her beautiful design.

"I'll just watch," I said.

My intended recipient and her husband are what I think of when I hear the term, "good people." Jim, an engineer, worked long days and came home to lovingly help in all aspects of dialysis without any apparent resentment. Kathy still worked for Hospice full time. When we stopped in at the local chapter one afternoon during my visit, the staff was quick to point out how much they loved her and what a wonderful person she is. I already knew this but I think the underlying message was that I couldn't have chosen a more deserving recipient for my kidney. She apparently hadn't told them her blood rejected mine so I just smiled and nodded.

The day before I left Kathy and I sat on the sofa in the trailer where they'd raised a daughter while building their retirement home. Outside the window three feral cats that she and Jim had caught and spayed before turning loose, stared at us from a safe distance while we looked through an album of old photos lain across both our laps.

When she flipped to the last page Kathy turned to me and through tears, said, "It hasn't always been easy, Ellie, but I've had a good life. A very good life."

Holding hands, we sat in silence as the afternoon light carried her words from the room with the quiet grace of a seasoned midwife.

***

As we readied to leave for the airport on my last morning I took the pink scarf from around my neck and draped it over Kathy's shoulder.

"Pink is the universal color of love," I said.

"I have something for you too," she said, disappearing down the hallway of the trailer. When she returned she opened her palm to reveal the hand-beaded pink necklace she'd made. I turned and let her fasten it at the back of my neck before spinning around to face her. We stood by the front door, our eyes swelling with tears, neither of us knowing what to say.

She brushed her thin brown bangs off her round face and smiled. "Thank you, Ellie," she finally said.

I threw my arms around her. "I am so honored to know

you guys."

When we arrived at the airport we were told my plane would be unable to takeoff in the dense fog.

"How far is it to the train depot?"

Jim glanced at his watch.

"Not far. I think we can make it in time."

We raced to the Amtrak station where I made it within minutes of the southbound bus leaving the depot. The bus wound through the redwoods for several hours before arriving at the depot where I could take a train the rest of the way home. I spent the twelve hours of travel time thinking about my time with Kathy and Jim and what it meant to me. When the train finally pulled into SLO I felt the full force of gratitude for my *one wild and precious life,* and most especially, my good health.

***

As the prospect of a paired match grew more unlikely, and having witnessed firsthand Kathy's challenging journey, I became determined to locate a donor for her. She had so much to live for: finishing the house, watching her new grandson grow up, helping people die with dignity and grace. Before that trip I'd rarely spoken to anyone about my plans to donate. Bragging about what you do diminishes the act itself so rather than talk about being a donor I'd preferred to blab about the needs of patients. I'd get embarrassed and more than a little uncomfortable when people would go on about what a generous thing I was trying to do. Their comments moved the focus off Kathy and people like her who are at the mercy of the rest of us.

Something shifted in me when I was up north. I often wore the pink necklace Kathy had given me and fingered the beads like a rosary, flinging prayers to unnamed angels in hopes that all her goodness might come full circle. And I started talking about living organ donation to everyone who would hold still long enough to hear me out. I talked about it in the grocery line, to spa clients, and to friends. I hoped that some of them, even just one of them, would be touched by Kathy's predicament and offer to be tested.

No one stepped forward. People seemed fascinated by the story but mostly just smiled and wished us well. I began to understand that what had been a fairly easy decision for me, was for most, too much to ask. I don't judge them because people do things all the time that I could never do. Like spending weeks in a tree to prove a point, for example. Joining the Peace Corps. Or choosing dialysis day after day, week after week, instead of just giving up and giving in to the inevitable.

***

As the presidential election neared I became obsessed with polls, checking and rechecking the various websites on a daily basis and reading political blogs until my eyes nearly bled. According to most experts the race was close and it was anybody's guess who might win. Of course the Democrats were sure their candidate was on top while Republicans insisted they had the election in the bag.

I volunteered at the local Democratic headquarters, making calls to voter lists and giving them directions to their polling places. When we needed someone to call the Hispanic voters, I convinced Jacob, who'd had four years of Spanish, to give it a try.

"Lo siento," he'd say, "Mi Espanol es muy mal!" We'd hear laughter coming from the other end of the receiver but he managed to get the message across, and I was proud of him for agreeing to help.

When election night finally arrived, a few close friends gathered at the coffee shop beneath the spa where a half dozen of us drank decaf and chewed our nails as the returns came in. We kept switching from CNN to MSNBC to PBS as we waited for one of them to call the race. Finally, it was Wolf Blitzer who uttered the words that made us all jump to our feet cheering and high-fiving each other as he announced that Barack Obama had won the election.

After hugging my friends goodbye that night I walked down to the beach by the light of the moon to where the waves crashed against the shore. Off in the distance seals barked raucously as if they too were celebrating. I stood looking out over the water and wept. Not because my candidate had won but because I'd just witnessed history being made as the first black President of the United States would soon hold the highest office in the country. I stooped down and picked up the first shell I found, putting it in my pocket to help me remember this night. Six years later I still have it.

SEVEN

November/December 2007

When I returned from my visit with Kathy and Jim it was to a busy new spa where my mind was set free from worrying about Kathy to focus on my friend Mary Kay's new business venture. I'd been accustomed to working with many of the same people month after month, year after year. With long term clients I could tell as soon as they walked up my driveway if they were out of sorts just by their gait or by the way one shoulder tipped forward. I adore my repeat clients but being at the spa offered the challenge of working on bodies with which I had no history. I imagine it might be similar to both the apprehension and joy an artist feels when standing in front of a new white canvas.

The other thing about working at the spa versus my private practice is that it was less solitary. Fortunately I had the privilege of hand-picking the massage therapists who'd be working with me. I pride myself on being able to discern between a person who can give a decent massage and someone for whom bodywork is a calling. One of the benefits of the interview process was that each applicant gave me a massage. Yeah, rough job, I know. I could usually tell within thirty seconds if they had the *gift* of touch that goes beyond education and training.

Like many massage therapists I began this career not by accident but by waiting. After spending a decade selling real estate in Michigan I realized that my job had evolved from helping people buy or sell a home into litigation prevention. When I started out, it used to be a showing, a friendly handshake, and a mutual signing of three, yes *three* documents over coffee in the broker's office. Over the years it had evolved into an hour-long ordeal with a stack of papers seemingly created in order to make buyer and seller suspect of one another and the Realtor fearful of overlooking a potential snag that could end up in a lawsuit. In short, it wasn't fun anymore.

When I became a single mom in 1990 I knew it would be difficult to support my children on the "maybe" of possible commissions, and it was. I kept it up for a while but when my broker offered me a position as administrative assistant I jumped on it. But the fit was temporary. There's nothing like a divorce to shake you at your core, rattle your demons from their cages, and set you on a search for more meaning and purpose in life. I'd always been a touchy-feely kind of person, very affectionate with my children, and likely to walk up behind my coworkers to rub their shoulders when they looked stressed.

The next month I'd enrolled in the massage program at Kalamazoo Center for the Healing Arts. Next door to the real estate office where I worked, the owner of a salon offered me cheap rent on a room to give massages to her clients so I could practice what I was learning. In the past, career transitions often felt like banging my shoulder against a brick wall. The switch from real estate to massage therapy was more like turning a corner and watching door after door swing open every time I approached, a huge welcome sign hanging over each entrance. I leapt through those doors with vigor, never looking back. A year later I was booked with massage clients nearly a month in advance. When my husband and I moved to San Luis Obispo in 1997 it happened again. I put the word out and the clients showed up day after day, week after week, until my practice was full again in a mere six months.

A few years later after becoming friends with one of the other moms at my son's charter school I approached her husband about offering massage at his Avila Beach inn. He not only said *yes,* he gave me a former service room to convert into a massage studio for his guests. When he opened a second hotel a couple blocks away I offered massage therapy there as well. A few years later they opened a coffee house and spa between the two hotels. Because I obviously couldn't and wouldn't compete with their new business I became a consultant on all things massage for the new spa, eventually transitioning to lead therapist when we opened.

It had taken 33 years of waitressing, selling houses, and raising babies for me to discover my true gift, one that had been waiting patiently in my hands all that time. Twenty years later my right arm has developed tendonitis and I tire more easily but I continue to see clients because I can't imagine where else I would turn when I need a healing. If I'm not able to receive I can always count on giving a massage to get the same results, because like they say, what goes around comes around. Nearly ten thousand massages later, I sometimes lose track of the coming and the going.

Time loses its linear righteousness during a massage, where flesh and spirit coalesce in perfect synchronicity. The massage room is my sanctuary. It is here that I am in my most perfect place and I become a vessel through which some unnamable thing passes. Sometimes it trickles out of my fingertips as I gently cradle a head. Sometimes it gushes forth as my hands glide from a foot all the way up and over the shoulder, then back down the arms where it's returned to me again, hand to hand. All I know is that eventually I end up at the foot of the table with my palms against soles, feeling exhausted yet energized. A sigh bolts from my lips, gratitude riding high on my breath.

When people ask if I attend church I say, *yes. Nearly every single day.*

I returned home from Kathy and Jim's to what was, in essence, my new family at the spa. Although many would come and go, these would be the people I'd grow closest to for the next five years. Not wanting to burden them with my personal struggles I'd told only a few of them about my plan to donate a kidney. From time to time one of the baristas or massage therapists would ask about the donation but as the months turned into years most of them forgot about it.

Or so I thought.

In mid-December we held our company holiday party in Avila Beach. We're used to our fellow massage therapists and baristas in tee shirts and yoga pants or jeans, so it's always fun to see each other all dressed up to the nines. Following the annual white-elephant gift exchange, Mary Kay stood at the head of the table smiling. She thanked us for our hard work and for being such happy part of her life.

Then she looked at me with that little gleam in her eye like she often gets when she's up to mischief and said, "Are you all wondering what I got you?"

We looked around at one another, puzzled.

She pointed at each of us and in her best Oprah impression, literally hopped up and down, shouting, "You get a kidney! You get a kidney! You get a kidney! Everyone gets a kidney!"

***

Jacob's birthday lands three days before Christmas and I'd pooled the two events into one gift, the thing every December baby will tell you they hate about being born so close to the holiday. Neither Jacob or I were big on spending a bunch of money on what had become a consumerist guilt-trip. Each year we'd agreed on just a small gift and spending time together doing something special like going to Yosemite for snowboarding and cross-country skiing or seeing a movie and getting dinner afterward. This was the year I broke our rule.

Because he'd attended boarding school for his first three years of high school, Jacob, unlike many teens, hadn't needed a car. Midland School was an environmental stewardship kind of place where classes were often held outdoors. Students lived in cabins and had to cut their own wood to light the fire needed to heat water for showers. Due to the needs-not-wants philosophy at Midland, Jacob never voiced a desire for a vehicle, other than to note that the ugliest car on the road was the Volvo and he felt sorry for people who drove them. However, driving Jacob back and forth to Cuesta College when he overslept or "forgot" about an exam was getting old fast so I tapped my friend Mary Kay for car-buying advice.

Her response was, "Whenever I see a young driver behind the wheel of a Volvo I think, *there goes a well loved child.*"

A couple months before Jacob's birthday I'd found a red Volvo station wagon on Craigslist for a really good price so I bought it. I figured if he hated it I would offer to trade him for my Dodge Caravan, betting he'd consider this social suicide and it'd be a win-win for me. The bright red car sat at the curb in front of our house for eight weeks but Jacob, who tended to live in his own world and was used to students parking up and down the streets of our neighborhood, never asked about it.

As we were returning from classes during finals week that December, Jacob was in a particularly down mood following a Spanish exam for which he'd been ill-prepared.

When we pulled into the driveway I said, "You want me to give you your birthday present early?"

He piled out of the van and looked at me.

"Um, *yeah.* Presents always help. What is it?"

I directed him to turn around.

"What?"

"There," I said, pointing.

"What?" he asked again. "I don't see anything."

It was all I could do not to double over laughing at my son, who not only had walked past the station wagon every day, but now failed to see it even as I pointed.

"There," I repeated.

His gaze narrowed to the car and his mouth opened as he slowly walked down the driveway.

"Wait...you bought me a *car* for my birthday?"

I followed him as his pace quickened, fumbling for the key on my chain. Jacob swung open the door and sat in the driver's seat, his hands on the wheel. I crouched down beside the car.

"I know you hate Volvos but..."

"Not *my* Volvo!" he interrupted. "Oh my God, I can't believe you got me a car. How can you afford—?"

It was my turn to interrupt.

"Shhh. It was a good deal. Don't worry about it. Besides, I'll teach you to drive so we'll save on that."

He jumped out of the car and threw his arms around me, his spirit instantly lifting as I handed him the key.

"Make good choices," I whispered into his ear for the gazillionth time. "And happy birthday."

A month later I got the call every mother dreads.

"I've been in an accident," he said. "Nobody's hurt but could you come?"

I found him only four blocks from our home where a truck had backed out of a driveway in front of him, its trailer hitch having plowed through the engine compartment of Jacob's car. Although a more experienced driver might have had faster reflexes I was grateful it wasn't legally his fault.

The other driver's insurance company wrote Jacob's car off as totaled due to the age so we shopped for a new one. He chose, I swear to God, *he* chose another Volvo wagon— green this time—a couple years newer than the red one.

Jacob doesn't much like change and takes comfort in the known. Plus, I think he witnessed just how safe that car was and understood now on a personal level the justification of driving a heavy tank when barreling down the road with only a few weeks experience behind the wheel.

As Jacob drove his second car off the lot I thought about Kathy and how she was a little like that slow but steady Volvo. Between hernias, angioplasty, and clogged veins from years of dialysis, you'd think she'd have given up and yet she still chugged along slow and steady, in it for as far as the road would take her.

EIGHT

Spring/Summer 2008

I lay under the skylight in my new but as yet unfinished addition listening to the rain and unable to sleep. I'd traded free rent in one of our rooms to a young contractor in exchange for building me a new bedroom so I could have more privacy. Ben was not our only housemate. I'd taken in a college girl while Jacob was away at Midland and recently moved her into my old room as soon as the new addition had a roof over it. Partly due to lack of patience and partly to lack of funds, I'd covered the studs with burlap and scattered rugs on the concrete floor to create a welcoming, if stark, room for sleeping.

Residing in a college town as expensive as SLO sometimes requires creative living arrangements, something any Cal Poly student who has slept in a closet or a shed or in a back yard tent will attest to. With Jacob graduating from community college I'd already promised his room to another student in the fall when he went off to university. For some people sharing your house with strangers might seem an odd thing. But we made it work, eventually even adding space in the camper from time to time when there were more homeless students than what our *urban oasis*—as the housemates called it—could hold. In the years since Jacob left for boarding school in ninth grade, a total of fourteen people have called this little house their home, some for a few months and others for several years.

As the rain pummeled the skylight I pondered the possibility of plasmapheresis, a process for washing antibodies from a donor kidney to counter rejection in the recipient. The procedure was the newest thing in the world of nephrology and Kathy had emailed me earlier in the week to tell me about it. She'd also reported a serious clotting problem with her needle site needed for hemodialysis that would likely require some sort of surgical implant.

Nearly a year had passed since we'd started and I began to worry more and more about her. Unlike most people, Kathy was difficult for me to read. I couldn't tell if she was more upset by health concerns or the fact that bears had eaten her chickens and coyotes had taken two of the feral cats she'd been feeding for several years. What I did know is that she was much more resilient than I ever imagined I'd be under similar dire circumstances. I wondered if her ability to accept difficult situations was what made her such a great hospice nurse or if dealing with death on a daily basis made her more accepting of her own fate?

I closed my eyes, hoping to quiet my brain and focused on the raindrops instead. Until suddenly it occurred to me that said rain was now coming *through* the skylight, dripping onto my bed, and splattering on the cement floor. I jumped up and loudly yelled, "What the hell?" before running to grab a stew pot out of the kitchen and place it under the drip.

Having heard my outburst from across the yard, a groggy Ben showed up outside my door to ask if everything was okay. Jacob wandered in a couple minutes later, as did our sleepy-eyed housemate. Together the three of us lay down towels and pans while Ben went up a ladder to determine what had caused the leak. He ended up throwing a tarp over the skylight and moving my bed to the opposite side of the room until he could get a better look at the leak in the morning. It was after four a.m. when they all returned to their rooms and I was left listening to the drip, drip, drip as each bubble of water exploded in the pan.

By the time daylight arrived I'd made my decision.

"I think we should try plasmapheresis," I said to Kathy. "I realize it might not work but I don't believe I'd be wasting a kidney if it doesn't. I'd rather try and fail than not give you a chance."

She was quiet on the other end of the phone. Kathy usually took her time when it came to speaking, thought out her responses carefully.

Finally, she said, "My doctor doesn't think I'm a good candidate. And it's such a new procedure that CPMC doesn't feel confident about trying it. I'd have to transfer to Cedar Sinai or some other big transplant hospital."

"Well then let's do it!"

"It's not that easy, Ellie. The insurance companies have to approve everything. And frankly I'm not sure I'm up to it."

"Just think about it," I said. "I'm willing."

"I know. Thank you."

"I'm sorry about your chickens and your cats."

"That's life in the boonies," she said. But I could hear a crack in her voice and I knew she was grieving more than she let on.

For the next several hours I googled everything I could find about plasmapheresis. The procedure had only a fair amount of success and mostly with patients more closely matched than Kathy and me. It was up to her whether or not she wanted to take the chance and if not we'd just wait until we found a matched pair at CPMC. It wasn't like my kidney was going anywhere and for now, at least, she was maintaining on dialysis.

***

The storm refused to let up and the downspouts had clogged with leaves causing water to pool in the yard. I pulled on a rain coat and rubber boots and headed outside. Too stubborn to ask for help, I dragged a heavy aluminum ladder to the side yard and propped it against the house. As the rain pelted me in the face I swept the roof and dug detritus out of the gutters. When my gloves became soaked I threw them off and stuck my hand down the spout, slicing my palm on a rusty edge.

Jacob walked into the kitchen as I stood over the sink with sopping wet hair, cleaning the wound.

"What's going on? Do you need some help?"

"You're a little late. While you were lying around playing X-Box I was on the roof in the pouring rain, cleaning out the gutters."

"Really? Because while you were up there being passive-aggressive, I was right here being straightforward and honest."

I wanted to be mad but I couldn't because he was right. In our ever-changing roles he was the mature one in that moment and I was acting like a crabby teenager.

***

An old friend once told me that whenever she was feeling sorry for herself, her mother insisted she go do something nice for someone to take her mind off her own problems. And if she got caught it didn't count; she had to do it anonymously. She called it the *pixie principle*. Every once in a while I'd find chocolate kisses or little bunches of wildflowers on my windshield that I knew meant my friend was having a bad day. But I felt conflicted because if I called her it meant she'd gotten caught, so I usually waited a day and then checked in. I also stole the idea and used it when I got caught up in my own tribulations.

A few days after my conversation with Kathy I set out on my monthly mission of "bottle bingo" to get rid of recyclables we'd collected over the past several weeks. Most

Californians are too lazy or too busy to turn in their mandatory-deposit bottles and cans for a refund. I am one of them. I piled two trash bags full of bottles and cans into the back seat of my Beetle and drove slowly through a neighborhood near the recycling center looking for a likely candidate. I usually found them rummaging through the garbage cans near Albertson's Grocery or riding a bike with a plastic bag slung over their back. Unfortunately I saw only students from a nearby housing complex and seniors from an assisted living center. Not willing to give up so easily I pulled into the parking lot and waited.

Less than five minutes passed before a short woman with a long braid down her back and a young girl of about nine walked by pulling a wagon filled with smashed soda cans. They parked the little wagon smack dab in front of my car and headed for the trash bin around the corner. I waited until they were out of sight and placed my two bags on the sidewalk next to their stash. I quickly got into my car and started to back out just as they returned. When she spotted my gift the woman looked around, confused. She left the bags and began walking away with the wagon.

As I watched it dawned on me what an idiot I was. In trying to preserve their dignity and my identity I'd failed to realize that there's a code on the street: you don't steal what someone else might have spent all night collecting in order to buy the next day's meal or a fifth of whiskey. Not even to feed your children.

I pulled back into my parking spot and jumped out.

"Wait!" I said. "These are for you."

The woman turned and stared, her mouth set in a straight line. The little girl pulled on her mother's hand and whispered something in Spanish. I set the bags down next to their wagon. The girl nodded at her mother, who picked up the bags.

"Gracias," she said.

"De nada," I said.

It wasn't long afterward that I stopped directing who would receive my bottles and cans, bringing them instead to the recycling center and asking the attendant to give them to someone who needed them most. I figured he knew the regulars and which of them had families to support. Once in a while I cashed them in and gave the receipt to the attendant as a tip for dealing with all those desperate faces day after day for minimum wage. In any case, I realized I didn't want the responsibility of choosing who would or wouldn't benefit from my small gift. I decided it was enough just to give them away.

On my way home from my botched episode of bottle bingo I listened to "Radio-Tradio" on a local AM station. I knew the host, Dave Congalton, from my journaling seminar days. About once a month he invited people to call in and sell their stuff or advertise for things they wanted. As I waited at a stop light it occurred to me that he had a wide and varied but loyal audience of local listeners and here was an opportunity to tap into that resource. I pulled into the Chevron station and parked in front of the air pump to dial up KVEC. When the producer took my call I gave her my nickname hoping Dave—who knew me as Eldonna—wouldn't recognize that it was me calling.

I heard a buzz and some static before Dave picked up my line.

"Here's Ellie in SLO. Hi Ellie. What can we sell for you?"

"Actually, I'm looking for something."

"Okay, what are you looking for?"

"Well, I know this will sound strange but I'm looking for a kidney for a friend of mine who is very sick and needs a donor."

"A kidney?"

"Yes. Preferably someone with B-positive blood although she can accept a few other types."

Dave hesitated and told me to send him an email because

he'd like to know more. At that moment I knew I was busted but I figured the pixie principle still applied because I wasn't trying to get caught. I was just trying to think outside the box.

I'd first met Dave at a writer's conference back in 2000. Unlike his robust on-air personality, Dave is a bit shy in person, a common trait among many performers from what I've learned. At the time Dave and his wife were co-directors of the conference and I'd offered to donate a massage certificate for the random drawing on the final evening. A few weeks following the conference I asked Dave if he'd have me on his radio show to promote my journaling books and he'd graciously consented.

Over time Dave has tapped me as a radio guest on several occasions. Between my appearances on his show to discuss local issues and our mutual love of writing we became friends, occasionally getting together for lunch. Following my call into his show that day I emailed Dave about Kathy's dilemma and he scheduled me to do a segment the following week. On air, I explained how 90,000 Americans are waiting for a kidney and seventeen people die each day because they didn't receive an organ in time. I spoke about how far the technology has come in terms of the surgery itself, as well as outlining the risks. And I begged for just one person to come forward to be tested.

After giving my spiel on behalf of Kathy, only a handful of people called in, mostly to commend me for my decision, however one caller thought I was loony for wanting to give away a kidney. I was gobsmacked to learn she'd undergone both a heart and lung tissue transplant herself. Another caller wanted to know who would pay for the costs. I replied that I was uninsured but the patient's insurance company always pays for the surgery and tests. Like others, she couldn't seem to grasp why I would take such a risk.

I left the studio feeling a little sad and a lot frustrated. Rather than giving me hope, the experience had served to underscore my gradual realization that I was the exception not the norm. I didn't want to believe that I was the only person who thought her life would improve by giving someone else a second chance at theirs.

My friend Mary Kay refers to this as my bodhisattva nature. The first time she said it I had to Google the word. In a nutshell, the story goes that the Bodhisattva is traveling across a desert where he passes groups of people who, like himself, are completely parched and near death. When he reaches a wall and peeks through a hole he sees a pool of water. Instead of climbing over the wall and drinking, he runs back to find each and every person to tell them what is ahead. Reading this beautiful story made me cry. It also made me even more determined to scour the sparse wasteland of potential donors for that one person who could save Kathy's life.

NINE

Fall/Winter 2008-09

The summer had flown by, partly because I was busy with work and a geology class, and partly because it's always those things you most want to savor that seem to slip away before you realize they're gone. Jacob had applied to five universities and ironically the only one from whom he didn't receive an acceptance letter was the one in our own back yard. But Cal Poly was on his shortlist only for reasons of convenience and financial consideration. It would've been a five-minute trip to classes and he wouldn't have rental expenses while living at home but the local college was not where Jacob would be likely to find his tribe. Cal Poly is home to many frat boys and sorority girls, engineering and Ag students, some of whom with parents who buy them a house to live in while they attend school.

We'd visited UC Santa Cruz during orientation and it clearly proved itself to be a perfect fit for my son. From recycled serving plates made out of potatoes, to the melting pot of international families, to dorms catering to gay, vegetarian, or drama students, the campus obviously supported individuality. When Jacob and I had looked out over the meadow to the ocean beyond the dorms that spring day UCSC reminded us a lot of Midland, the John Muirish boarding school he'd attended for his first three years of high school. The Santa Cruz campus had been designed around the landscape rather than the other way around. The students and staff greeted us with smiles everywhere they passed us, often stopping to ask if there was anything we needed. And the Language Studies program—a sub-section of the linguistics department—was rated one of the highest in the nation. In essence, it was exactly what Jacob was looking for.

We'd returned home from UCSC stoked about his registering for fall classes. Getting used to living in a house without Jacob after being nearly joined at the hip for twenty years would take some adjustments. It helped that I was already sharing my home with a college student and another tenant in the granny unit next door. Not exactly an empty nest. It also helped that he would be less than three hours away.

One of the hardest days of my life was the day we crammed all Jacob's stuff into my van and tied his bicycle onto the roof. Backing out of the driveway, I pointed the van toward Highway 101 and watched as our little pink house disappeared in the rear view mirror. Four long hours later we landed in Santa Cruz and unloaded everything into a room he'd be sharing with two people he'd never met. As I began emptying boxes and hanging clothes in his closet he put his hands on my shoulders and turned me to face him.

"I appreciate your help, Mom, but I've got this."

"I like helping! At least let me make up your bed."

He took the sheets from my hands and tossed them on the bare bunk then put his arms around me.

"Thank you for everything. I wouldn't be here if not for you."

I cried like a little girl most of the way home. A week later I received an email from my son in response to my asking how he was adjusting to college life. He wrote, *What's not to like about waking up and rolling out of bed to walk through the redwoods in sandals where I have to stop and let deer cross the path on my way to class?* Clearly he had found his place and the community that supported it. I was beyond happy for him which helped to counter my sadness at not having him home.

Within a couple months of Jacob's leaving I started feeling antsy myself. The thing about transition is that it comes with wheels. You might feel as if inertia has planted your feet in clay but external forces don't give a flying freak about feelings. When the winds of change begin to blow you either have to lean into them or give yourself over to indifference. In December I'd be finishing up my studies at Cuesta College, adding another associate's degree to the collection of certificates in the drawer.

When I enrolled in classes I didn't really have a specific educational goal other than rounding out my business and healing arts background. I figured at best I'd end up with another associate's degree and the possibility of eventually working toward a B.A. At worst it would be good mental and social stimulation and I'd end up with a little more knowledge than when I started. Either way I'd be forty-nine by the time I finished so I had nothing to lose. Yet even before finishing my current program I started wondering what might be next. A road trip? A new business venture? Join the Peace Corps?

Behind all these questions lay the greater uncertainty of if and when the organ donation would take place. So far Kathy and I had not been favored with a matched pair. She'd recently confided in me that she held out little hope, knowing that only three percent of the population shared her exact blood type and antigen combination. Three percent! In addition her brother Bob, who'd received a kidney a few years prior, had developed a brain tumor and died in July a mere six months after his diagnosis. Kathy explained that the immune suppression drugs make transplant recipients vulnerable to invasive diseases.

Added to all this, Kathy's health was not good. She was scheduled to undergo PKD-related surgery and had been suffering from fatigue. In her most recent email she suggested that I consider donating instead to her younger brother Ralph who also needed a kidney. It would have to be another "paired match" as he was a different blood type, but he didn't have her antigen issues so we'd be more likely to find a match. *I understand that you were hoping to donate to me*, she wrote, *but quite frankly I don't know if my gut would be able to handle all the pills I'd have to take for immune suppression following a transplant. Just think about it, okay?*

I didn't have to think for very long. It was obvious from her email that Kathy was becoming less and less invested in a kidney transplant as her health declined. As much as I'd grown to love her I decided that paying it forward to her loved one was the best gift I could probably hope to offer. I contacted her brother whose transplant team quickly sent me the now-familiar set of vials.

"We've got to stop meeting like this," I said to Annika as she filled another tray of blood tubes.

"You are one determined donor," she said, after I'd explained the move to test for Kathy's brother.

"Determined or stubborn? I'm not completely sure."

***

Once again I found myself in limbo as I waited for the results of my blood typing with Ralph. My restlessness was unwavering and I eventually determined it to be more a factor of menopause than any desire to travel or start a new venture. The more I read up on the symptoms the more I realized that my edginess and feeling unsettled had to do with my physiological state rather than my emotional one—although the latter was also affected by erratic changes in hormones. I would be fifty in a few months. Living, working, and going to school with twenty-somethings had created a bit of an illusion of youth. I felt younger simply by proximity to all that vitality and vigor. But my body knew better and it didn't hesitate to remind me with hot flashes, irritability, foggy thinking, weight gain, and insomnia.

At forty-eight, I was just beginning to grasp the relative nature of one's age. As far back as I can remember, I always thought my parents were old. My mother was a dozen years younger than my dad. Like me, she went back to college to finish her degree when her youngest child was Jacob's age. My father, on the other hand, was likely born old. He had an old walk, old ways of thinking, and an old heart that was as weak as it was warm. Despite my dad's heart condition and my mother's comparative youth he outlived my mother by thirteen years. Mortality, it seems, isn't determined by our habits so much as it is by fate and good genes. Just ask the ninety year-old woman puffing on a cig who never walks further than her mailbox as the healthy vegetarian drops dead mid-stride on his morning jog past her porch.

I no longer believe age is about the state of one's health or a measure of years so much as it becomes a more authentic way of living. Having felt the piercing gash of grief and lived through it, having loved to the brink of brokenness, and having learned the difference between friendship and frivolity, one eventually takes a conscious step through the invisible membrane that separates hubris from humility. This event is not marked by a certain age so much as it is an uncertain promise of tomorrow. As I push my way through the late- summer years of my life, I'm learning that older people don't slow down because they have to so much as because they choose to.

After Jacob left for Santa Cruz, a few well-meaning friends suggested I consider online dating, that maybe it was time I found a loving companion to fill the void left by the last child going off to college. But along with the other symptoms my libido had not gone unaffected and I had no desire to date. I assured my friends that I rather enjoyed my own company, thank you very much, and for the time being I was happy to lean into the next decade as a solo participant.

The more I considered my restlessness the more I

realized that instead of waiting I should continue living my life in ways that brought me joy and fulfillment. And so I did. Rather than signing up for a dating service I joined the YMCA in an effort to give my body and its resident kidneys the healthiest possible home while I incubated them until such time as surgery would occur. Apparently I'd forgotten that I hate gyms. I despise the grunting, sweaty, disco-beat energy and mirrored weight-lifting rooms where I become hyper-focused on the size of my drooping backside.

The only class I could tolerate was aqua-aerobics and only if the air temperature was warmer than the 80-degree outdoor pool. This rarely happens in temperate San Luis Obispo. Luckily I found my way to an evening class in the super-warm therapeutic pool with mostly-older women. The ladies were funny and friendly and I eventually came to call them my friends. I didn't lose weight but the aqua-aerobics class gave me a needed boost both physically and emotionally and I was grateful for this. As autumn leaned into winter I looked forward to those nights when, week after week, we jogged in circles through chest-deep water as the sun crawled behind the surrounding mountains.

***

In early January I received a desperate email from my friend bree, who always spells her name with a lower case *b*. She pleaded with me to participate in an upcoming production of *The Vagina Monologues*. When he was a student at Cuesta, Jacob did part of his work-study under the drama director which led to me seeing almost every play bree produced. Our frequent contact eventually led to her becoming a friend and massage client. As much as I wanted to keep busy with extracurricular activities I called her to explain that although I was flattered by her request, I was no actress.

"That's the thing. You don't need to be," she assured me.

"Yeah, but I don't think I can memorize. Menopause has short-circuited my brain capacity."

"No memorizing, you just have to read. I need a couple more people or they're going to cancel the class."

It bugged me that the arts always seemed to be the department that was picked on when it came to cancelling classes due to budget constraints. I was familiar with all the great work that writer and activist Eve Ensler had done with victims of sexual abuse and I knew the production was for a good cause. Plus I wanted to support bree.

"Okay," I finally said. "I'll do it."

"Great! I'll send you a permission code to register along with a list of rehearsal dates and times. It'll be fun, you'll see."

At the first meeting a dozen women of varying ages sat in a circle discussing the different monologues and voicing preferences for which piece they wanted to read. I chose one about birthing titled, *I Was There in the Room.* As the mother of a doula and having attended a few deliveries besides my own three, it felt like a good fit.

One of the other monologues had to do with different types of orgasms and I was beyond relieved when the lesbian next to me volunteered to read *The Woman Who Liked to Make Vaginas Happy.* However, bree decided to select different women to be the "voice" for each described climax, doing an eeny-meeny-miny-mo type of assignment as she rattled off our names to correspond with varying orgasms.

When she pointed to me, I swear to goddess, I heard her say, *"The surprise triple orgasm."*

As soon as our meeting concluded I literally ran up to bree and told her that I could not possibly act out said triple orgasm on stage let alone in front of these women.

"Sure you can," she winked. "You just don't know it yet."

"But..."

Before I could finish my sentence she'd already engaged

set designers and lighting techs, leaving me standing in the wings, script in hand, pondering the limits of friendship.

As it turned out bree was right. I have no idea how or why but at the second or third rehearsal I just decided to go with it. I let loose with a low growl, followed by a squirming high-pitched squeal, and topped off with a bouncing grunt-fest that shocked myself as much as it did bree. When I lifted my head the women were applauding and bree was howling.

"Yes! Yes! Yes!" she shouted, and I realized that I did indeed have it in me after all.

We put on three performances and although thankfully I couldn't see out into the audience with the bright lights on our faces, I recognized bree's cacophonous laughter and knee-slapping approval at every single show. Having shown up for his many drama performances, Jacob agreed to attend on one of the nights he was home from Santa Cruz. Following the show he remarked on how pretty I looked on stage and congratulated me on how well I'd read the birthing piece. But he admitted that he absolutely could not look up during the orgasm bit and might have even covered his ears.

***

A week or so after my first and last stage debut I received an email from Kathy's brother Ralph. Although grateful for my offer, he now had a donor and wouldn't be needing my help after all. Despite being happy for Ralph, I felt as if I were in kidney-limbo again, held hostage by Kathy's health and the statistical improbability of finding a matched pair. This news, juxtaposed against my unrelenting desire to accomplish what I had set out to do, left me feeling extremely conflicted.

As if she could read my thoughts, Kathy called the next day to ask if I'd be open to a visit from them in April. She and Jim had planned a small vacation to Yosemite on the way to see their daughter and grandson. Because they'd be fairly close, she thought it'd be nice to swing down to see me. The rooms in my house were full so I arranged for them to stay in one of the condos above the spa where I worked in Avila Beach.

The fact that Kathy was feeling well enough to travel was encouraging, but between her compromised health and her brother no longer needing me as a donor, I was feeling a bit pessimistic about the donation. Even if the registry hit on a paired match, which was highly unlikely, there was no guarantee Kathy would be healthy enough to undergo a transplant. I did my best to let the process flow but I wasn't getting any younger and knew the older I got the more difficult the recovery could be for me. I hoped that seeing Kathy and Jim again in person would help me make the difficult decision of whether or not to stay plugged into my intention to become a living donor.

I was busy working in the spa when Jim and Kathy arrived and checked into their beach-stay apartment. After finishing with my last massage client of the day I climbed the stairs up to their unit and knocked on the door. Jim gripped a loop of rubber tubing in one hand like a lasso as he reached around me to close the door.

"Hi, Ellie! It's great to see you!" He smiled and nodded toward the living area. "Kathy's a little tired from the car ride."

I joined his wife on the sofa where she was already prepping her left arm for the evening's dialysis with the portable machine they'd brought along in a wooden crate. Jim had painstakingly designed and built the box for travel purposes. I leaned in and kissed her on the cheek.

"How are you feeling?"

"I'm okay" she said, but I knew from the lack of color in her face that she was probably overdue for a blood cleanse. "How were your massages today?"

"Really good. I love what I do."

We chatted a bit while Jim checked on his delicious-smelling stew between rigging the machine and setting up the needles and gauges. He unrolled a tube and stuck one end into the bathroom sink just as a knock sounded at the door. I jumped up to answer it and was met by a former coworker of Kathy's who'd stopped by to say hello.

"Hi, I'm Arthur*" he said, reaching out to shake my hand. "You must be Ellie."

"Good to meet you," I said. "Please come in."

Unfazed by the mechanisms of dialysis, he stepped over the tubing to hug Kathy then handed Jim a bottle of wine. He gazed toward the ocean where the setting sun reflected pink dabs of light over the water.

"Wow. Nice digs! Do you live here, Ellie?"

"I wish. I live in SLO but I work in Avila so I feel like I get the best of both worlds."

Arthur plopped down in a leather chair facing Kathy.

"It's been a while," he said. "How've you been?"

Kathy briefly summed up the current state of our donor dilemma before changing the subject to their shared past. I listened as the two nurses exchanged stories about their time working together. Hearing them laugh in the midst of her treatment helped buoy my spirits. Thanks to the wine and the food and the company I went from feeling melancholy and disheartened to optimistic, happy and full. As I drove toward home a couple of hours later I thought about how honored I was to know these amazing, resilient people who laughed and joked through what would put most of us into a deep funk. When people would call me a hero for wanting to donate a kidney I told them about Kathy and Jim and the countless others for whom this is their life. To me, they are the true heroes.

The following day the three of us made a trip to a local market called Avila Valley Barn. Jim and Kathy stocked up on tapenade, pickled veggies, fresh fruits, and various cheeses. Knowing that Jim has a thing for old train stations I drove them around the area a bit, ending up at the Amtrak depot in SLO. Kathy waited in the car while Jim and I ambled between old wooden benches to the tracks behind the station. As we stood on the landing, Jim turned to me and smiled.

"Thanks for this, Ellie. It was nice of you to remember."

Kathy and Jim needed to get back to their suite early that evening to rest up for the five-hundred mile trip home. I dropped them back at their car where we'd met earlier in the day. As the three of us hugged each other at the side of the road, tears met tears. I think we all knew how this was going to turn out. Although we felt sad about the likely outcome of my intended donation, we shared a sense of gratitude for having gotten to know one another through the lengthy process. If the transplant center had asked me to fill out the donor questionnaire that day I would have without question listed them as family.

In the days after they left I began to doubt my own judgment for undertaking what seemed like such a fruitless effort to be a good samaritan. It was looking less and less likely that Kathy and I would be able to find a paired match and that the donation would ever become a reality. For someone who defines herself as an optimist I felt a visceral shift of faith in the probability of my original intention to become a living donor. Maybe there were better ways to affect change than donating an organ. Maybe I should give up on the idea altogether and just move on with my life. And maybe Jacob was right to question my sanity for embarking on this crazy idea in the first place.

PART TWO

TEN

Spring 2010

Three years had passed since I'd signed on to be a kidney donor and although technically still in the paired match program with Kathy, I found myself revisiting the Matching Donors website from time to time. Fortunately most hospitals had changed their rules to allow unrelated donors. As I scrolled through the profiles one afternoon I kept coming back to my original intention to alleviate the prolonged suffering of another human being. Knowing the diminished probability of being Kathy's benefactor I decided to reach out to one more patient. This time to an environmental policy consultant in Washington, D.C. named Alice.

I heard back from her almost immediately:

Hi Ellie! I'm so grateful to people like you who are out there offering themselves to others - thank you so much. I'm a woman who has had kidney failure most of my life. I've been on dialysis (awful) and have also had two transplants from family members. These both lasted a long while but they eventually do fail over time, even when you are taking good care of them. So now I'm very sick, close to resuming dialysis, but hoping to avoid it. I am highly sensitized so I will likely have to ask a lot of people to be tested before I find someone with whom I may be compatible. I'll send you my profile as well and give you a call later today. I hope you will consider getting tested to see if we might be a match. Many thanks! Alice

Well, there it was, that imaginary ball flung back to my side of the net where it landed squarely between empathy and inertia. As I reread the email from Alice I thought about Kathy and Jim. I thought about how close we'd grown and how potentially devastating it might be to lose yet another failed donor match. And yet I also knew that as a hospice worker she was well aware of the profound reality of her illness and the likelihood that we'd never find a matching pair.

When Alice and I spoke on the phone the following day she sounded weak but cheerful. She told me a co-worker was also being tested but due to her antigen sensitivity, the more potential donors the better. I shared with her my prolonged journey with Kathy and my quandary in terms of loyalty. Alice assured me there was no pressure from her end and that she'd be grateful if I were willing to be tested to see if we were a good match.

I decided to go ahead and have my blood tested—my fourth round at Sierra Vista Hospital—where the technicians were now familiar with the pink-pigtailed lady and her tidy pack of vials. When I walked back to the phlebotomy cubicle a week after my phone call to Alice, Annika greeted me with a smile.

"More blood?" she asked, as she handed me a ball to squeeze while she readied the tubes.

"Another patient. The first one wasn't a match and the second and third ones found donors who lived closer to them."

She inserted the needle painlessly and unleashed the rubber strap on my upper arm as blood coursed into the first tube.

"You are a woman on a mission," she laughed. "I get the feeling when you set your mind to something you're pretty much unstoppable, right?"

"I suppose so," I said, despite feeling less and less

resolute as time passed.

She printed my name on each tube and carefully placed them in the shipping container.

"Maybe this one will be it, huh?"

"Maybe," I said.

She smiled and tilted her head to one side, her long, thin arms crossed in front of pastel printed scrubs.

"You're a good person, Ellie. I see a lot of sick people every day and it's people like you who help keep me from feeling overwhelmed by the unfairness of it all."

"Thank you, Annika."

She pulled off her latex gloves and put her hand on my shoulder.

"Thank *you*."

I hopped on my vintage 3-speed and headed down the sidewalk. As I pedaled toward home I found myself studying people as they went about their day pumping gas, pushing a grocery cart, or standing at the ATM. I couldn't help but wonder how many of them might know one of the ninety-thousand people on the transplant waiting list, or worse, had lost someone who'd died before receiving a needed organ. As frustrated as I was with the process I knew it paled in comparison to the struggles of the folks on that list. For the time being I remained committed to donating. Maybe not to Kathy and maybe not to Alice—maybe not even this year. But someone out there was eventually going to hear the words they'd been desperately waiting to hear: *We have a kidney for you.*

***

At some point during the previous year SLO County began work to rebuild a small bridge that passes over a walking trail before it joins the main road to Avila Beach where I work. The resulting detour required an additional five minutes drive time. Despite the inconvenience of having to leave a few minutes earlier to reach the spa, I enjoyed the new route. That extra stretch of road took me past a wooded resort, a hot springs, the Avila Valley Barn, and a ramshackle frame of an abandoned building that seemed to defy nature from every angle.

Something about the way it stood so proudly, rotting posts like crutches under the arms of a sagging roof despite its obvious near-death status, drew my gaze every time I drove past. I felt an odd kinship with this freak of nature, understood on a cellular level how it feels to defy gravity—stand steadfast with feet planted firmly on one's foundation even when the rest of you leans into certain fate. I've seen it in myself at times but mostly I've recognized it in people like Kathy or Alice, who've drawn the short straw in life's gamble for precious time on this earth.

Over time the weathering of wind and sun through aging timber moved me so much that I finally pulled over to photograph the old barn while on my way to a massage. The appointment was for a couple who were spending the man's last remaining days near the ocean. He'd been sick for some time and when medical and spiritual methods failed to stop the cancer from spreading, they'd finally made peace with the inevitable. Rather than grieving impending death they'd decided to celebrate the end of his life with massages, wine-tasting, and hot springs as self-prescribed treatments for a man keening toward his own grave.

Ivan's smile preceded him by several yards. He was older than his wife by at least twenty years and there was a sort of grace in that. I wanted to believe she'd eventually find love again.

"Right this way," I said, as I led them to the changing area.

We heard laughter on the other side of the door where he and his wife slipped into robes before their spa services. He joked with us as we soaked and scrubbed their feet in colorful bowls of hot water. The wine-tasting had made them a little silly but the laughs didn't feel like they came from a bottle. Rather, they seemed to bubble up from a childlike place within the depths of a man who'd suddenly been freed from the constraints of societal expectations. Watching him I understood what it means to care more for one's true nature than the nature of manufactured propriety. I found myself laughing throughout an event that could easily have been awkward and sad.

Inside the candlelit treatment room I gently cradled Ivan's bald head in my hands before starting the massage. Under the sheet he looked almost like a corpse, so thin and frail. But when he opened his eyes and smiled I no longer saw a dying man but a human being, someone's lover, someone's brother, someone's baby. Behind those wizened pupils lay a silent plea for a blessing which I happily obliged as best I could. As I massaged his cancer-ridden body he sighed softly, his face the picture of bliss. For the next hour Ivan and I danced in perfect synchronicity as the shadows flickered around us. I ended at his feet, doing a "this little piggy" along his toes before quietly slipping out of the room.

When Ivan emerged he threw his withered arms around my massage partner and me, pulling the three of us into a voluptuous group hug.

"I love you!" he shouted.

As he paid for their massages I complimented his colorful sweater.

"Would you like it?" he asked.

I'd have taken it had it not been so brisk an evening and had he not been so thin and obviously in need of warmth, but we both knew what was unspoken in that offer.

A moment after they walked out the door I discovered he'd left behind his St. Christopher's medallion and raced down the sidewalk to return it. He thanked me and winked as the irony of a saint on a chain passed between us. I watched them disappear up the street feeling grateful to be part of the fiber of his story as he untangled himself from the tapestry of this life.

The following weekend the county was hit with a major storm. It took down trees, knocked out power, overflowed creeks, and caused mudslides up and down the coast. I railed against the wind and rain, hoeing the back yard to create a trench for the water to drain off. I set plastic tarps over the skylights and caulked around the patio doors. Despite my efforts water seeped into my tenant's bedroom, the roof leaked, and rain found its way under the slider. When the power went out I was forced to stop fighting and give into the experience instead. I lit candles, listened to the wind howl through the trees, and hoped for the best.

Having moved to the central coast from the Midwest, for me a little precipitation wasn't a big deal. Unlike earthquake-nervous Californians I'd grown up with the terror of Mother Nature above me rather than below. One could look up at the sky when it turned a pinkish shade of gray and feel the atmosphere become thick with foreboding. I remember how humidity hung in the air just waiting for permission from above to let loose. People spilled out of their houses onto front porches and lawns. Farmers and townsfolk gazed up at the ominous clouds, scanning the horizon for telltale funnels. Children stopped playing, fear curdling the lunch in their bellies. The landscape transformed into a still photograph, the kind that has faded to yellow. This was the quiet that preceded "weather." It could be a severe thunderstorm or a bout of pounding hail but in our guts we all thought *tornado*.

As a young girl I felt the power in our collective fear of twisters. At our rural elementary school we practiced tornado drills, guaranteeing a new generation of storm-phobics. When we'd huddled under desks until given the "all clear" from the principal, I felt sorry for the kids who sat against the far wall. One of them was chosen each year to be responsible for opening the windows to ward off implosion. Every fall on the first day of school I took great care in choosing my seat.

On any given day from June forward, long before cell

phones and Internet, somebody would tell somebody else that a tornado cloud had been sighted. Immediately children weighted down with blankets and board games were shuffled down basement stairs or into storm shelters. The adults carried radios and a few probably had a flask hidden in their overalls or apron pocket. I don't remember now which corner we were supposed to take refuge in, the one that would offer us the most protection.

We'd huddle together in our musty-smelling basement armed with Monopoly and Scrabble to keep us occupied. The rain fell in dollops outside, filling the window wells with muddy water. My mother kept her ear to the radio listening for news of the impending storm. Eventually Dad would come scurrying in from his office across the street as my sisters and I passed the time sneaking past Boardwalk and trying to scare each other. Every once in a while my father would creep up the back stairs for a peek at the threatening sky. We'd wait quietly for his return, shivering at the howling wind that vibrated the basement windows.

One of my older sisters told me that a tornado sounds like a train roaring overhead. Fortunately for us that frightening sound had never punctuated the safety of our cellar. Although I sometimes felt afraid I took comfort in the fact that we were all together—a rare thing in a family of nine—and I knew that if we were going to die we'd be going together so I didn't feel I had all that much to lose.

Eventually the world outside our basement windows would become quiet again and we'd head upstairs to gawk at the aftermath of the wind's fury. We'd discover the occasional car demolished by a fallen tree, power lines down, roofs missing shingles. The day's weather would be the topic of grocery line conversation for weeks afterward. Until November, when the sky turned dark once more and the word *blizzard* passed ominously from mouth to mouth.

The day after the California storm I took the shorter route to Avila now that the new bridge had been completed.

When I arrived at the spa the manager mentioned that Ivan's secretary had called, questioning the spa charges on his account the previous month. The "secretary" turned out to be his widowed wife, meaning that the woman with whom he'd shared his last days must have been his mistress. I didn't know whether to be sad for the wife or happy for Ivan. I made a note to look him up on the Internet later to see if he was mentioned.

On my way out the door the receptionist remarked about the old barn on Avila Drive having blown down during the night. She'd seen me photographing it on her way to work the week before and thought I'd want to take an "after" picture. I set my phone on the front seat so I wouldn't forget to take the longer route home, but at the last minute I turned and crossed the new bridge instead. I decided I'd rather remember the beauty of a keening barn than a pile of wood on the ground, a living man's cacophony of laughter over a dead man's pithy obituary.

ELEVEN

Summer 2010

I finally heard back from Alice. She wrote to say that although I was a very good blood match the transplant team in D.C. had chosen a co-worker to be her donor. Alice thanked me emphatically for my offer and asked me to stay in touch and I promised I would. On one hand I felt relieved not to leave Kathy in the lurch but I also wondered if I might actually be preventing her from finding a viable donor. What if there were a matching kidney out there with her name on it but because she was attached to me in the paired program she'd never know? As someone who tends to over-think things it was difficult not to obsess about the maybes and what-ifs.

Fortunately summer was my busy time work-wise and work, for me, is the perfect distraction. Doing massage in a resort area means being available within thirty minutes of receiving a text from the spa desk, as opposed to the winter months when I'd be texting *them* just to see if my phone was still working because business was so slow. With work picking up I got further and further behind on the weeds and maintenance so I looked forward to Jacob being back for the summer to help with chores around the house.

"When do you expect to come home?" I asked him a couple of weeks before the end of spring quarter.

"Actually I'm thinking of Summer School. There's a

program in Mexico—"

I didn't even let him finish his sentence.

"You're not going to Mexico! It's dangerous there!"

"Mom, only the border towns are dangerous. I'll be with a teacher and a large group of students at the Universidad de Cuernavaca. It's safe."

"But…"

"I need the credits. And it'll be good to do an immersion program."

Jacob was legally an adult but he'd still need me to fill out forms and sign papers for the parent loan to cover the gap in costs. The thought of something bad happening to him scared the crap out of me but I also knew that he needed to break loose and start getting out into the real world. By saying no I could be holding him back from an extraordinary experience. Like I said, I tend to over-think things.

"You're sure it's safe?"

"*Mom.*"

"Okay. I'll fill out the papers. But I'm worried."

"You always worry. And it always turns out okay. You need to trust me."

I trusted him, I just didn't trust the world *with* him. He loves collecting insects, playing video games, and when out and about almost always gives people the benefit of the doubt. And coming from a small town he wasn't exactly what one would call street savvy. Combined, I knew these traits could make him a target for those who would take advantage of his generous nature. But I also knew he was a smart kid and I needed to have faith in his abilities to figure things out for himself.

I snapped a photo of Jacob as he stood in line with a backpack slung over one shoulder, wearing his signature corduroy blazer while waiting to have his papers checked at LAX. He'd tucked his head of curls under a newsboy cap earlier that morning and I wondered if the TSA would pull him aside. On the day he'd had the passport photo taken he'd combed his hair out into an afro so huge it looked square after the picture was trimmed to fit the page.

Jacob handed his passport to the uniformed woman who studied it, then him, then the photo again before looking up and waving him through. As he disappeared through a winding queue of travelers I contorted myself trying to catch one last glimpse of my son before he was swallowed into the masses. I stood a while longer before heading back toward the parking lot. When I finally located my car, I sat inside and bawled for half an hour before driving out of the garage.

Six weeks later Jacob arrived home from Mexico unscathed so far as I knew. It would be months later before I learned that he'd had a gun held to his head as he and a friend walked back to their room one evening. According to my son, three young men had followed them after noticing a couple of gringos wearing backpacks. His friend wasn't very fluent in Spanish so Jacob did the talking. He'd asked the thieves very calmly just to take the bags and let them go. The bandits grabbed the packs and yanked a pair of headphones off my son's neck before running off into the darkness.

Although his friend lost an expensive laptop, cell phone, and a camera in the robbery, the thieves were probably disappointed and perplexed by the "loot" from my son's backpack. Jacob laughed as he described what a letdown it must have been to pull a collapsible bug net, a jar containing dead insects, and an entomology field guide along with a Spanish textbook from his pack. Surely they must have resented this particular American even more than before they robbed him.

Jacob's Mexico tale had a lasting impact on me. For weeks after hearing about it I had nightmares about the robbery. Each time I would wake up in a sweat, then feel a huge surge of relief upon realizing it was just a dream. It terrified me to think I'd nearly sent my child to his death by signing those papers. *What if...?* I kept asking myself, circling back each time to the realization of how thin the veil is between life and death, between this world and whatever, if anything, comes after it.

Especially for people like Kathy and the ninety-thousand others on the organ transplant list, many of whom are mere steps away from that dark alley where death does not hide in the bushes but stalks them right out in the open, just a few paces behind. What is it like for those mothers and fathers, those brothers and sisters, those husbands, wives, and lovers to accept that probable fate?

My logical brain tells me that we're all going to die one way or another so who am I to think I have any control over the inevitable? Millions of people choose to live on levees knowing they are destined to flood or in mobile homes smack dab in the middle of tornado alley. Millions more of us have plunked ourselves down within miles of a known fault line, seemingly oblivious to the probable "Big One" that's likely to occur any day.

Despite all my friends telling me I was crazy for moving to where my house could crumble without any warning I'd only experienced one earthquake since moving to SLO. It was December 22, 2003, Jacob's fifteenth birthday, when I rolled a blue recycle bin up the driveway and noticed our camper shaking and rattling. My first thought was that a couple of horny college kids had sneaked into the trailer to shag in privacy. But then I realized the earth was swaying beneath my bare feet. Remember those carnival fun houses where you have to walk across a shifting floor? It was kind of like that. Only much louder.

When the ground stopped shuddering I was more shaken by my new awareness of the powerful forces within the planet than the quaking itself. I felt something loosen in my core along with the side-slipping faults, something akin to a false illusion that I am in control of my life. For weeks afterward I carried with me a heightened sense of how small we are in the grand scale of things.

Anthony De Mello, a Jesuit priest and psychologist once

said, "Enlightenment is absolute cooperation with the inevitable."

I suppose most of us are not enlightened then, because we become dearly attached to the people we love. Our happiness is often inextricably chained to their presence in our lives. Although I might agree with De Mello that I should accept reality, it doesn't mean I can't play a part in how that reality unfolds. Of course we are all going to die, some of us sooner than others. By choosing to donate a kidney I don't proclaim to be saving anyone's life. What I hope is that I'm offering the gift of a postponed departure rather than a pardon from the inevitable. The kidney will benefit the eventual recipient but the gift is equally for those that know her and aren't yet finished loving her in this lifetime.

***

Unlike Kathy, who visits her grandson every couple of months, it had been almost two years since I'd seen any of my six grandchildren. So after finding a cheap ticket online, I flew back to Michigan during the last week of August. My oldest daughter Andrea had found a cabin big enough to hold both her and her sister's families at a campground not far from where they both lived. We hadn't told the kids that I'd be coming because we wanted it to be a surprise.

The secret got out to Andrea's children but when Maggie and her kids arrived at the cabin I hid in the back bedroom. Her oldest child was the first to find me. He threw his arms around my neck and shouted, "Grandma!"

I rubbed his blond crew cut and kissed him on the cheek.

"It's so good to see you, kiddo."

His younger sister had been a kindergartener the last time I saw her. She watched from a distance as her brother greeted me before sitting next to me on the bed. Within moments she moved her hand over mine and held it.

"I don't know you," she said, looking up at me from

under auburn bangs, "But I know that I've missed you." She leaned her head on my shoulder as the baby of the family, now six, jumped up on my lap to join the reunion. I felt like a grandma sandwich and it was glorious.

We spent the weekend roasting weenies, playing in the pool, dawdling on the porch swing, and going on a hayride while getting reacquainted with one another. The days flew by and I was reminded that the biggest price I've paid for living in California was not the cost of real estate but the inability to see my kids and grandkids more often. By the time we drove out of the campground in two minivans that Sunday afternoon we were all a little less clean but a lot closer to each other.

Before returning to California I met with my sibs in a restaurant at a halfway point between most of their homes. I'm the only one who ditched the cold snowy winters. The rest of my five sisters and brother live within a 100-mile radius of one another. When the seven of us assemble in one place we make a lot of noise, mostly laughter. These rare get-togethers remind me of those days we gathered around our dining room table every Sunday after church. We'd wolf down pot roast and watch my dad's skinny tie inevitably dip into the gravy bowl as it passed from hand to hand. Our parents are gone and we're all much older now but our personalities have followed us into adulthood. My eldest sibling is still the quiet one, the next one down the witty one, beneath her the sweet one, next-older-to me the smart one, my younger sister the shy one, and my baby brother the silly one.

I sometimes wonder what *one* I am to them. As we stood in the parking lot outside the restaurant I mentioned this to my brother, with whom I am probably the closest and have shared the most details of my life. Possibly over-shared, if you ask him.

"You're definitely the free-spirited one," he said, laughing.

Had I asked when we were younger I'd probably gotten an answer like the rebellious one or the restless one, but age has gifted us with more respect for one another's individuality. According to Webster *free-spirited* means someone who thinks and acts without being overly concerned with social norms. It's a rather pleasant way of saying impulsive and careless but given the multitude of answers he could have offered, I'll happily take this one.

***

I felt a bit melancholy as I watched the flatlands and pine trees disappear beneath the airplane wing the next day but it felt good to head home. Jacob returned to Santa Cruz to begin his senior year at UCSC the first week of September. He'd decided to move off campus and share a home with a couple of other students. While he was schlepping his thrift-store furniture across town I was moving back into the granny unit where he and I had first lived when I'd purchased the house almost a decade before. I rented out my bedroom to a Cal Poly student who joined two girls already renting rooms in the main house. I left my washer and dryer in the house but reserved rights to use it, not just because I didn't want to go to the Laundromat; I knew I'd miss seeing their bright, sometimes sleepy, usually happy faces on a daily basis. Doing laundry in the house gave me an excuse to look in on them.

The downside to renting rooms was that being a mom, maintaining a professional boundary between landlady and tenant created a challenge. If I heard a siren, for example, I immediately stopped to review a mental checklist of "my girls" and whether they were in class, at work, or home. It was Jacob who had urged me to take over the small attached studio instead of sharing the house with three young women.

"You're the landlady not the house-mother," he'd said one day when I'd refused to raise rents to cover the rising property taxes and utilities. "It's too easy for them to take advantage of your kindness when you're bringing them food and giving them rides."

I knew it was good advice but I resisted.

"What if I get lonely?"

"They're right next door, Mom. You deserve your own space."

Moving back into the granny unit turned out to be a great decision. There's something about claiming one's space that feels almost bulimic—as though you've been stuffed with all these extra shoulds and hold-backs and then suddenly you just let it all out, take up every inch of the room with your own breath. I'd forgotten what it was like not to worry about waking someone if I wanted to grind coffee beans early in the morning or not have to wash someone else's dishes to get to the sink. I loved those girls but Jacob was right. I deserved this. And I discovered that not only was I not lonely, I reveled in the solitude.

TWELVE

September/October 2010

I clipped a flannel massage sheet onto the clothesline with
two wooden pins before putting the transplant coordinator on
speakerphone so I could continue hanging laundry while we
talked. Lana had called to tell me about new program through
the National Kidney Registry, an organization that hoped to
broaden paired donor searches via a computer.

"Will it increase our chances of finding a donor for
Kathy?" I asked.

"Statistically, yes, because we'll be trading information
with other transplant hospitals whose patients might or might
not be on the UNOS list. In other words, we'll be trying to
match you two with patients and donors whose information
we've not yet had access to. People who could potentially be
a match for Kathy and you. But there are no guarantees."

"Do I need to do anything?"

"We'd need you to be completely cleared for transplant
prior to putting your information into the program, so yes.
You would have to have all the pre-op tests and more blood
tests, of course."

The wind stirred various sets of chimes into song. I
flipped the empty laundry basket over and sat on top,
switching Lana back to my ear so I could hear her better.

"Can I have the tests done here in SLO?"

"Most of them but a few have to be done in our labs here

in San Francisco."

I fingered the necklace Kathy had given me on the day I left after my visit to her home, mindlessly rolling each bead between my thumb and forefinger.

"Let's do it," I said.

"Okay, Eldonna. I'll let you know as soon as I hear anything."

I set the phone in my lap and closed my eyes. A damp sheet whipped into my face and for a moment I couldn't breathe. Embedded in the scent of sun-dried linens I caught a nostalgic whiff of my mother, me leaning against her legs while I handed her clothespins as a little girl. I miss my mother every day but there are times when the wishing pushes itself into an ache. What I wouldn't have given to have been bestowed with her insights as I pondered the consequences of decisions I felt unequipped to make.

I couldn't talk to my mother so I did the next-best thing. I dialed up Eloise.

Eloise was one of my very first SLO clients. She sought me out after a chandelier had fallen on her head. Yes. On her head. The first time I saw her she was getting out of the passenger side of a white Cadillac, all four-feet-eleven of her. Wearing a blue striped top over white pants and sporting perfectly-coifed red hair, she carried herself like a woman twenty years younger, despite the neck injury. Her 83 year-old husband Glynn removed his hat and nodded at me politely from the driver's seat.

"I'll just wait here and read until she's done," he said.

I reached through the window and shook his hand.

"We'll be just half an hour."

While filling out the intake form Eloise made it clear that her doctor had recommended massage therapy, lest I think she was the type who spends money on wasteful pampering. As if seeking treatment for pain after a chandelier falls on your eighty-one year-old noggin is a luxury. Like me, she and her husband had moved to California from the

Midwest, a clue to her apologetic comments. Back East (that's what they call anything the other side of the Rockies over here) people are taught to always put themselves last. Self-indulgence is the tenth deadly sin, right after cutting in line and not blessing a sneeze.

I helped Eloise undress, noticing how she cringed every time she moved her head. As I gently worked through the layers of tension in her neck I assured her she'd done the right thing by scheduling a massage. By the third appointment I'd convinced her that half an hour wasn't long enough to address eighty years of life's toll on the body of a mother, teacher, and farmer's wife, and she happily agreed to extend her treatments to an hour.

Over the next decade Eloise became much more than just a faithful client. The friendship we shared was more like a favorite aunt or godmother. I grew to know all her grandchildren by name and she watched Jacob grow from a small boy to a young man, always remembering him on birthdays and holidays. Her husband Glynn packed a paper sack filled with peppermint candy, nuts, fruit, and homemade cookies for me every week. And every week I'd pretend not to notice he'd fallen asleep in the car while reading his dog-eared copy of Louis L'Amour.

Although both amazingly sprite and clear-headed for their ages, over the years Glynn started taking a lot more naps and Eloise's balance became increasingly unsteady. Worried she might fall while trying to manage my steep driveway, I convinced her children to buy a massage table so I could treat Eloise in her home. Store-bought biscotti replaced the home baked cookies in my parting treat bag. Eloise, who has long prided herself on remaining self-reliant through her eighties, now let me clip her toenails and pluck the occasional stray hair from her chin. Even Glynn's stoic facade faded some and he would let me hug him before I left.

I'd come to dearly love these two precious human beings. On a rational level I understood that the closer we became to each other the closer they moved toward their eventual departure from this life. I realized every kiss on Eloise's soft cheek at the end of her treatment could be my last, each lingering wave from the living room window the closing frame on a favorite movie.

"I love you, Honey," Eloise said, after her last massage before they moved six hours north of SLO to be closer to their daughter. "Don't forget your goodies on your way out."

"I love you, too," I said.

Glynn stood nearby while I folded up the massage table and tucked it into the hall closet.

"You'll like that biscotti," he said. "It's chocolate."

When I turned to face him it was as almost as if those old eyes could see through my fragile smile straight to that most tender place in one's being. In an uncharacteristic act of unspoken love he not only let me hug him a little longer than usual, he opened his arms even before I made my move.

Five years later, Eloise and I still keep in touch over the phone. As I sat in my back yard after Lana's call, I told her how much I missed having Jacob around and filled her in on the latest details of what was going on with the donation. I shared my frustration about how the kidney donation had morphed into a roller-coaster of disappointments.

"You always strive to do the right thing but Honey sometimes you just have to let things happen the way they're supposed to."

I already knew this but took comfort in hearing it from my dear friend as much as if it had come from my own mother's mouth.

"We'd sure love to have you up for a visit," Eloise added. "You know you're always welcome any time."

Four days later, as the first rain of the season fell on the central coast, I packed up my yellow Beetle and headed toward Lincoln, California. I slept in the guest room of Eloise and Glynn's beautiful new home in their neatly-groomed retirement community north of Sacramento. Eloise was nearly as spry as ever, leaping up to fetch things for her ailing husband almost before he finished his sentence. Glynn, on the other hand, had slipped considerably since the last time I'd seen him and spent most of his days in a recliner.

For her ninety-third birthday I gave Eloise a massage, the only gift she would accept from me. As my hands ran over her body it felt familiar but changed. She'd lost weight and the outline of her spine had become like pebbles on a crooked path.

"Are you eating, Eloise?"

"My appetite's not so great."

"You need fuel to maintain your strength."

Normally I don't talk during a massage, preferring to let a client relax and go to their quiet place but it was always different with Eloise. We laughed a lot and she enjoyed sharing stories. Sometimes we told each other secrets, many of which made us both cry. On this particular day she confessed that as much as she loved her husband, waiting on him these days was no easy task. I made her promise to let the home health workers act on her behalf even when Glynn preferred his wife do the things she'd always done for him.

After her massage I filled a bowl of water and set it on a towel at Glynn's feet. Despite refusing my many offers to put him on the table I'd often sensed that he felt a little envious of his wife's massages. This time, however, he gave in and allowed me to give him a pedicure. I scrubbed his feet with sea salts and massaged up to his knees, then carefully trimmed his toenails before gently slipping on his socks and shoes. By the time I emptied the water bowl he was sound asleep, mouth agape in a half-smile.

Three days later I pointed my VW back toward SLO, wondering how much longer I would have Glynn and Eloise in my life. Both were several years older than when my father had died. Although Eloise appeared mostly healthy I knew it was only a matter of time before I got the call and I was already dreading it. They'd become my family and the loss, when it happened, would leave a big fat dent in my heart.

Six hours on the road is a long time to think about life and death. I turned on the radio to drown out my thoughts but the only receivable stations in the central valley are Spanish or country western. I chose Spanish because I didn't want to listen to a bunch of sad cowboy stories but it didn't matter. Although I couldn't understand a word of the language I knew the Latin ballads were all about the same thing: *love*. Finding it, keeping it, losing it, and hoping to find it again. Eventually I turned off the radio and drove in silence, preferring the hum of my wheels on the road to the melancholy music as I drove home.

When I finally pulled into the driveway and dropped my bags on the floor, the first thing I did was check my messages. The results were in: no matches for Kathy and me. None. Nil. Zip. It was our last best chance and we'd once again ended up with an empty hand. Due to less than three percent of the population matching Kathy, our only options would be to hope for a miracle, or call it quits.

I don't remember who called whom the next morning but the conversation was one of the most difficult I've ever had before or since.

"I'm sorry," I said. "I feel like we've tried everything."

"It's okay, Ellie. Don't feel too badly about it. I didn't have my hopes up much knowing the odds."

I sighed.

"I wish I could say the same but I'd be lying."

"We're grateful for everything you've done, Ellie," Jim chimed in over the speakerphone.

"Hi Jim. I know. This is all just so difficult. I never thought it would take this long or be this hard."

A pregnant silence filled the five hundred miles between us before Kathy broke through the discomfort.

"Look, you've been unbelievably patient and generous. Why don't we just take a break from thinking about this for a while. How's Jacob? How's work going?"

I did my best to make small talk. But in the back of my mind I wrestled with the fact that as I edged closer to the far side of menopause I became less inclined to subject myself to major surgery. Practicing massage for twenty years has taught me that the older we get the longer it takes the human body to heal. I wasn't saying it aloud yet but I could feel my spirit sink with the realization that I probably wouldn't be able to help Kathy. Having grown to love both her and Jim, the thought of letting them down nearly broke my heart.

We wound up our conversation and said our goodbyes as cheerfully as possible but as soon as I clicked on "end call" I almost threw up. Before I could fully absorb the weight of my disappointment the phone rang again. It was Lana from CPMC.

"Hi Eldonna. How are you doing?" Lana's voice was always even and I could never tell whether she was about to relay good or bad news.

"Hi Lana. Well frankly, I could be better."

"I'm sorry about the news regarding you and Kathy. But I have a proposal for you."

"I'm all ears."

"Now that CPMC is partnered with the National Kidney Registry, and because you've already completed most of the tests and are good to go in terms of surgery, how would you feel about a non-directed donation? We could put your information into a broader search for a compatible match with a random recipient."

"Non-directed donation? You mean let the computer choose a complete stranger?"

"Exactly. I recently heard of a chain of transplants that went nine deep all because of the first non-directed donor."

"Nine? Really? That's amazing. But how would that affect Kathy?"

"Well that's the thing. We'd move Kathy into a pool of hard-to-match patients who'd get first priority should a cadaverous kidney become available. It's not a promise, but it would definitely increase her odds."

"Wow. This is all pretty overwhelming."

"I understand. You don't have to give me an answer right now. Just think about it, okay?"

"Okay. Thanks, Lana. I promise I will."

With the sudden change in the direction of my altruistic path I felt like the earth had just shifted beneath my feet. I'd initially decided to donate to a stranger I'd chosen based upon their alignment with my beliefs about what it means to be a good citizen of the world. Donating to a *random* stranger immediately triggered control issues around knowing who my organ would benefit. And yet an enormous sense of surrender hung right there within my grasp. The relief surrounding it was almost palpable.

As I considered Lana's proposal I realized that not only should I not be the one to decide who would get my kidney, the responsibility of making such a decision was a burden I didn't necessarily want anymore. No matter who would receive my kidney, saying yes to one meant saying no to others. Over the last four years I'd found myself becoming emotionally invested in the lives of those who'd brushed up against my own. The more I considered the opportunity that Lana was proposing, the more I understood what a huge gift she was offering me. Despite feeling terrible about the prospect of abandoning Kathy, relinquishing attachment to the outcome of my donation liberated me from an illusion of control over the situation. No matter how much I wanted to help Kathy, I knew in my heart that I had done my best and I was pretty sure she knew it too. I called Lana the next day and gave her the go-ahead to sign me up as a non-directed donor.

***

As the donation process had slowly progressed I began to get a bigger picture of just how insidious kidney disease is and how many people are affected by it. The more I learned, the more grateful I was to be born into a family where although we'd lost our mother to bone cancer at age sixty-four, my siblings and I have enjoyed relatively robust health. According to the National Kidney and Urologic Diseases Information Clearinghouse (NKUDIC) one in ten American adults suffer from some form of chronic kidney disease. Coming from a family of nine, we'd missed being a CKD statistic by exactly one.

You might be wondering why I'd go so far out of my way to donate a kidney when this disease didn't affect anyone in my immediate family. Why not bone marrow? Or why not just donate my time instead of one of my vital organs to someone I don't even know? These are all perfectly legitimate questions; however, my motivation wasn't born out of logic so it's difficult to explain.

But I'll try.

I believe we are all equal beings. Wealth might make you comfortable but it can't save you from eventual death. Education might keep you from poverty but it can't prevent disease. Geography might help protect your civil rights but it can't protect you from unpredictable tragedy. Where we're born and most of the opportunities we're born into all come down to chance. Some disease is generated by bad habits like smoking or diet, some is environmental like chemical exposure or lack of available prenatal care, and some is just wonky DNA.

Perhaps one day science will figure out how to prevent or cure a lot of the diseases that are inherent in our society. I recently heard NASA has invented a 3-D printer that can print "food" for astronauts so it doesn't take up valuable space. Maybe printing a human kidney isn't that far off. But for now, beyond one's belief in a higher power, all we have to sustain our hope is the grace of our fellow human beings to help us through our struggles.

A logical or left-brained person might look at the data, decide the evidence is overwhelming against self-sacrifice to aid others, and leave it to politics or science to determine another's fate. And here is where I invite Captain Obvious into the conversation to state that I am not left-brained. In fact I am so right brained that I sometimes wonder why my head doesn't rest on my right shoulder. I'm a touchy-feely, tree-hugging, artsy-fartsy human being who truly believes we are all brothers and sisters in this world, and that by helping one person you help the collective. I believe each of our deeds, good or bad, creates a ripple. Birth might be about circumstance but life is about choices within the events that occur year to year, day to day, and most importantly, moment to moment.

The encounter with Lucy might or might not have been chance—I don't know. Had I not moved to California with my son, had he not attended Cuesta College, had I not chosen one class over another, I never would have met her. What looks random in the immediate moment might seem like fate for those that believe in predestination. For me, it was merely an encounter with another human being who raised my consciousness about a particular form of suffering and I chose to act upon it.

Am I a hero or am I a fool for my act?

If my donation makes a positive difference in the life of one recipient and his or her loved ones, wonderful. If it creates a chain reaction of transplants, awesome. But if it helps you, dear reader, to also consider organ donation, then that makes you another beautiful pebble in the center of a magnificent ripple. And I have no doubt your generosity will undoubtedly overlap other lives in ways you can't imagine.

THIRTEEN

November 2010

In addition to being in good physical condition one must be deemed mentally stable in order to be eligible to donate a kidney. Shortly after my conversation with Lana, a medical advocate and ethicist not associated with the hospital contacted me for an independent interview.

Her first question was easy.

"Is anyone pressuring you to donate?" she asked.

I laughed.

"Actually, just the opposite. Most people think I'm out of my mind for undergoing unnecessary surgery." As soon as the answer was out of my mouth I regretted it. I'd just told the psych lady that people think I'm nuts. "I'm doing this of my own choice," I added.

She didn't say okay or hmm or respond in any way so I hoped I hadn't failed from the get-go.

"Have you ever been diagnosed with a mental illness?"

That one was a tad more difficult. In response to a couple challenging events in my past, I had experienced associated depression. But those down periods were acute episodes that responded well to making some important life changes.

"No," I said. Because I didn't want to have to explain what I knew was in the past and not a barrier to being a donor.

"How does your family feel about your donation?"

"They're concerned, of course, but they support my decision."

Frankly, after three and a half years had passed since I'd first signed up I didn't think any of my family believed it would really happen. I hadn't talked about it much when everything stalled and they probably assumed I'd changed my mind.

"Has the hospital informed you of all the risks, including possible death, from this type of surgery?"

My mind shot back to the day of my initial consultation with the head nephrology surgeon at CPMC. Using a primitive sketch that he drew on a blank sheet of paper, Dr. Bry had explained how many organs and systems were involved in removing a kidney. They could conceivably damage anything connected to or in the way of their mission—from my pancreas, to my adrenal gland, my spleen, my intestines, or even my other kidney. I was also, they'd said, subjecting myself to possible infection. My heart could stop. I could have an allergic reaction to the anesthesia. And if they nicked a major blood source I could bleed out in a matter of seconds.

It had been a sobering interview but I remained steadfast in my decision. Statistics were very much in my favor and I am an optimist. Or mentally deficient. Which is likely the reason they hire this lady to determine one's mental and emotional state, given the possible outcome for something that is completely elective.

"Yes," I finally answered. "I understand the risks."

"Okay. And you realize that in this program you are allowed to have a voice with regard to whom you donate, right?"

"The transplant coordinator already explained that I could limit the parameter search," I said. "I told her I'd prefer they looked for someone fairly close to my age or younger so it might provide a longer life for the recipient. And that I really hope this ruled out Dick Cheney."

It was the first time the interviewer's voice broke from professional propriety.

"You said that?" she laughed.

"Yeah. Not very enlightened of me, was it?"

She didn't answer but I could tell by her little coughs and deep breaths that she was having a difficult time composing herself for the next question.

"Do you have anyone to take care of you after surgery?"

"My son Jacob."

"This is major surgery, Ms. Edwards. You'll need help walking, using the toilet, bathing, food preparation, and dispensing medications. How old is your son?"

"He's 21. Almost 22."

"Have you thought about hiring someone to come in for a week or so to help you?"

I hadn't thought of it and even if I had I wouldn't be able to afford it. The recipient's insurance pays for travel to and from the hospital, labs, and the hospital stay, but not for aftercare. They don't cover lost wages either so as a self-employed single mom I would have to trust that people would show up to help.

"I think we'll manage just fine," I said, because I'm fortunate to have good friends.

Take Lisa, for example, who the following day got up early in the morning to drive me to my colonoscopy appointment. Lisa was one of my charges in my role as lead therapist at the day spa and we often jokingly told people we were mother and daughter. Both blond and originally Midwesterners, we'd bonded on our respective moves to the "Left Coast" and separation from our families over 2000 miles away. I added her as my daughter on my local YMCA membership and she listed me as her mother on Facebook.

Lisa is, in fact, a lot like my own daughters. She is kind but has an irreverent sense of humor. She once mooned me during a tandem massage knowing I was the only one who would see her ass-crack and that I would have to struggle to keep my composure. And at a clothing exchange party I'd thrown, she returned from the bathroom wearing every single barrette, flower, and headband she could find, nonchalantly strolling through the living room waiting for us to notice. It was the kind of thing no one expects from a sweet, soft-spoken girl from Minnesota but that I have since come to learn is the thing I love most about Lisa.

Like most bodyworkers Lisa is also generous and compassionate, and immediately offered to chauffer me to and from the local medical center for my 8:00 a.m. colonoscopy. She accompanied me inside the doctor's office to give the nurses her contact information and hugged me before she left.

"I hope you don't fart in the doctor's face," she said, loud enough for everyone in the waiting room to hear before striding out the door.

"That's my daughter," I said, blushing.

I took a seat among the snickering group of starving, rectum-burning patients in the reception area. Most of them had likely spent the previous night making repeated trips to the bathroom, thanks to the god-awful solution prescribed to empty one's intestines prior to the procedure. I, on the other hand, felt cheery and well rested because I didn't drink the stuff. After researching the harsh ingredients and reading up on exactly why it's prescribed, I decided to take a gentler more holistic route.

For four days preceding the colonoscopy I ate only soup. Three days out I ingested a natural colon cleanser purchased from my local health food store. And on the last day I drank only fruit and vegetable juices. I also scheduled a colonic for the evening before the surgery, which entails a gentle enema with abdominal massage to remove any residual waste product from the colon. It just seemed a lot gentler than downing chemicals that are potentially toxic to one's kidneys right before they remove one of them.

It wasn't my first colonoscopy so I sort of knew what to expect. I've always had problems with my guts. At the age of forty, after trying everything from colonics to hypnotism to Metamucil (which my grandfather used to call *metamusical*, having no idea how funny or apt it was, given the side effects) I finally gave in and saw a medical specialist. When I'd asked the internist about the difference between a sigmoidoscopy and a colonoscopy, he'd just grinned and said, "About seventeen inches."

The procedure itself wasn't that bad, thanks to a nurse friend who'd tipped me off on how to get enough Versed, a drug that makes you madly drunk while mercifully erasing the memory of the entire event. When asked if the drug was working I simply answered that I didn't feel any different despite the fog creeping in on the edge of my consciousness. They gave me another shot, after which I have no memory of the camera-on-a-stick that turned my body into a recumbent popsicle, other than the vague awareness of a reality TV show displayed on a huge screen, starring my colon.

During the follow-up visit the internist presented me with stills of my short-lived reality show and announced that I have a *lazy* colon.

"Yeah, well you're a lousy photographer!" I shot back, waving his blurry photographs of unidentifiable body parts..

Where did he get off telling me my intestines were too lazy to move on schedule anyway? Maybe I had better things to do than sit around in the bathroom waiting for a peristaltic response to dinner. Like find out where I can get more of that Versed stuff, for instance. I've got a few more memories I'd like to erase.

Ten years later when I came stumbling down the hall after my second colonoscopy, Lisa was waiting with a hot cappuccino. I took a sip and nearly lost my balance.

"I'm just gonna hold up this wall while you sign the release papers, okey-dokey?"

Lisa drove me home then held my arm to steady me as

we walked up the driveway.

"Don't forget to drink your water," she said, throwing a blanket over my drunk ass after I flopped onto my bed.

"I love you," I mumbled, as drool already started to pool on my pillow.

By the time Lisa closed the blinds and let herself out I was out like a rock.

Sometimes we tell people we are mother and daughter. What they don't know is that sometimes we swap those roles.

***

Next up was the mammogram. Confession: I am not someone who gets them regularly. Despite all the pressure from the medical community and the fact that at least half dozen women in my outer radius of friends have been diagnosed with breast cancer, I remain unconvinced. It seems that smashing breast tissue could make one more susceptible to damaged cells that might become more vulnerable to invasive diseases. Perhaps one day the technology for early detection will improve but for now I prefer monthly self-inspection.

As I changed out of my pink tee shirt and into the front-tying gown in the radiology lab I thought about all the women, all the breasts, all the news—good and bad—that originated in this tiny cubicle. I thought about my sisters. I thought about my well-nourished babies. And I thought about my own mother.

Up until my youngest brother pushed his way into our already-crowded house of six girls plus two parents, I hadn't taken much notice of the difference between my chest and my mother's, or even my oldest sisters' developing bosoms. As a five year-old I assumed the matching bulges that filled my mother's dresses were God's way of gifting warm pillows to sleepy heads as they nodded off on soft laps. This all changed the day my grandmother stood over our kitchen table sprinkling starch-water on sheets and pillow cases while my mom rocked the newest addition to our family in her arms. To my utter amazement, my mother unbuttoned her blouse and pulled the swaddled lump that was my baby brother against her bare chest.

I watched in awe as David latched onto her nipple and suckled for all his 13-pound worth (yes, that was his birth weight!). My mother and grandmother continued chatting, sometimes in Dutch. I didn't understand why neither of them considered this fat-cheeked new person currently gumming my mother's breast to his heart's content wasn't worthy of wide-eyed staring.

Dumbfounded by the extraordinary event taking place in our kitchen, I moved closer to my mother in an attempt to get a better look but the edge of her blouse concealed both her boob and my brother's face. Undaunted, I planted myself in the adjacent chair, then matter-of-factly reclined until my head was in my mother's lap. I lay under the arm that supported the slurping baby where I had a dead-on view of this most curious happening. Sure as Sunday, David was sucking on the end of my mother's breast. As if that weren't impressive enough, my mother pulled her nipple out of his mouth and flopped him over her shoulder, leaving the pendulous pillow dangling above me where—I-shit-you-not—warm, bluish-white milk *sprayed* my face.

I jumped up and wiped my cheek with my sleeve as my grandmother cackled in the memorable way that is forever etched into my bones.

"Whatsa matter, *meisje*? You want some?"

I shook my head emphatically.

That laugh again.

"Sure you do. Give her a taste, Aussie.".

A warm heat traveled up my neck and over my face. In a moment more surreal than I had yet to experience in my short life, my mother pulled me closer and placed my small hand on her bare breast.

"There's milk inside. It's how the baby gets his food. Same way you and all your sisters were fed."

Still recovering from the blasphemy of bodily fluids that had just anointed my face, I was completely flabbergasted by all this new information along with the sensory input of my mother's breast under my palm.

As if sensing my thoughts my mother smiled and nodded.

"Go ahead," she said, "squeeze."

I looked down at the hand that no longer registered as part of my own body and curled my fingers around her flesh. It was the warmest, softest thing I'd ever touched in my life. When I squeezed, milk bubbled out from her big brown nipple and onto my mother's aproned knee.

My baby brother belted out a burp, breaking the suspended silence.

"Atta boy!" my grandmother said. "Let that air go, it ain't payin' rent."

My grandmother moved a basket of damp linens to the steaming mangle in the corner of the kitchen. Tucking her breast back into her bra, my mother dropped the other one before shifting my brother to the opposite side. I left a room filled with hissing and suckling and my mother's low humming, changed by the extraordinary events I'd just witnessed. As I climbed the stairs to my bedroom I carried with me a new understanding of how much my mother loved us and her mother loved her.

A nurse called my name, startling me out of my reverie.

"Are you okay?" she asked, noting the tears I'd just wiped with the hem of my sleeve.

"Yeah, I'm okay," I said. "It's just a routine scan."

FOURTEEN

November 2010 (continued)

After almost four years of mostly waiting for something to happen, I now found myself in the midst of a medical whirlwind. Between the colonoscopy, the mammogram, EKG, and blood tests, I'd gone from nearly giving up on the donation to becoming hyper-focused on it. A little distraction was in order and thanks to my dear friend Nick, I found it.

I'd met Nick and his wife at a New Year's dinner shortly after we'd arrived on the west coast. Like us, they were looking to make friends with similar-minded folks in the area after moving to California from the Midwest. Coincidentally we'd been seated at the same table and soon discovered all four of us were transplants from Michigan with corresponding interests in environmental, spiritual, and humanitarian activities. Unfortunately, as often happens, when Bill and I split up in 2000 we drifted apart from our "couples friends" and I'd lost track of Nick and his wife.

It had probably been seven years since I'd seen Nick when he spotted Bill and me having coffee one afternoon at Steynberg Gallery, a cafe that hosts local art shows and intimate concerts. My ex-husband and I had managed to remain friends after our divorce and would occasionally get together to catch up on the other's life. Nick sat with his men's group reading and discussing Dante' as they apparently did every Tuesday.

A huge smile spread over Nick's face as he strolled over to our table.

"Bill? Ellie? It's so good to see you!"

We both stood and enjoyed one of Nick's gregarious hugs.

"You look great, Ellie. Are you still doing massage?"

"I am. And still loving it."

He glanced back toward his friends who patiently waited to start their reading.

"Give me your card. I don't want to lose track of you again."

As I fished around in my backpack he turned to Bill.

"Are you two..."

"No, we're just friends," Bill said, saving him from the awkward question.

"Ah. That's great."

A week later Nick met me at Joe Momma's, the coffee shop below the spa in Avila Beach where I worked. We immediately fell back into our familiar friendship and promised not to lose touch again. Since that day we've shared hours of great conversation and many dinners followed by shared poetry over a cup of tea and dessert. Our relationship is platonic but our love for each other runs deep. He is the kind of friend with whom I can share anything and not feel judged, be completely my silly or serious self and feel totally accepted.

On the evening after my mammogram, Nick and I met up at Steynberg to enjoy a concert given by an up-and-coming gypsy band of seasoned local musicians who call themselves Café Musique. Their music is both lively and haunting and the banter between the members made us feel as if we were sitting in one of their living rooms. Every chair was filled and people clapped and tapped their feet while the band played a variety of songs for nearly two hours without stopping.

Near the end of the concert the familiar notes of *La Vie*

En Rose tumbled from the stage and the audience quieted—except for one. The words, beautiful and tender, drifted toward my ears from behind me and I turned to discover a white-haired gentleman clutching his wife's hand, head tilted back and eyes closed as he sang. I don't speak French but I didn't need to understand the words to translate the feeling. It was as if an angel had landed in the middle of the concert. Many, if not most of us, were moved to tears as he sang.

We all have times in our lives where we think, *if I died today, right in this moment, I would die happy.* This, for me, was one of those moments. Surrounded by people, many of them familiar faces from other concerts and gatherings, my dear friend next to me, and music that penetrates the heart, I was completely blissed. Sharing such a beautiful moment I felt certain that other people all over the world were sharing similar experiences. Perhaps even those hooked up to a dialysis machine.

***

Exactly eight days from the day I'd agreed to become a non-directed donor, Lana called again.

"We have a match, Eldonna. A really good match."

"Already?"

Although I'd initially thought that Kathy and I would have been several years beyond our surgeries by now, after the drawn-out wait I just assumed it would take much longer to find a match for my kidney. When I caught my breath I asked the first question that came into my mind.

"Who is it?"

"I can't share personal information but I can tell you it's someone in New Jersey. And as of right now the NKR shows the chain four surgeries deep. His wife—"

"So it's a man?"

"Yes, and his wife is donating in order for him to be eligible to receive your kidney. That's how the chain works."

"I see."

"It looks like the next domino will fall in Chicago and then another in San Diego. But you never know, it could go further if the last person's donor is still waiting to be matched."

"Oh my God. It's really happening."

"Well, we're still waiting for the final blood re-matches and labs but yes, it could happen soon if you're amenable."

"How soon?"

"That's up to you. Once we schedule your surgery the rest of the hospitals down the line will schedule theirs. But we could feasibly do your transplant next month."

I ran through the dates in my head. We were already coming up on Thanksgiving. Jacob would be home over Christmas and New Years if I needed him to help during my convalescence.

"How about the second week of December?"

Lana paused as she looked through her surgery calendar.

"We can do 4:00 P.M. on Thursday, the sixteenth. Will that work for you?"

"Hell if I know," I laughed. "But let's plan on it."

I hung up the phone and promptly sat down on the floor. Bella rose quietly from her bed in the corner and padded over to stand next to me. She licked the tears from my face as I quietly wept into her silky ear.

***

Once the reality started to settle in I became even more focused on details, starting with the last test that could be performed locally: the pelvic exam. I hadn't had a pap smear in several years and I'd put it off until last because I dreaded it. Due to an extremely touchy cervix I find the procedure painful and anxiety-inducing. *Lady Exams,* as one of my friends likes to call them, are right up there along with colonoscopies and dental visits on my list of Things-I-Wish-

I-Never-Had-to-do-Again.

I decided to walk to the nearby clinic thinking it might be a good way to calm myself before the appointment. After learning the docs were an hour behind schedule I sat in the only chair available, next to a teenager with blonde roots sprouting beneath her dark ponytail. She rested her cell phone on the bulge beneath her tee shirt as her black-polished fingernails danced across a slide-out keyboard. Knowing from experience how hard it is to raise a child at such a young age I felt sad for her. Sadder still when a toddler joined her from the toy-corner and began running a broken truck along her thigh.

As much as I try to live my life in the moment, sitting in the reception area of the clinic was one of those times when I started wishing I had the ability to fast-forward a few hours. In my experience most waiting rooms are depressing, but this particular one reeked of pain and poverty and I found myself sitting on the edge of my chair as if it wouldn't be upwards of an hour before I left it. I glanced at the pile of magazines on a nearby table, wishing I'd brought a book from home. I'm not interested in celebrities; I don't even know who *People's Sexiest Man of the Year*, Ryan Reynolds, is, let alone care why other people think he's sexy.

My grandmother used to say I had no "sittenagot" or some such thing, a Dutch phrase meaning I couldn't keep still. I was often at the receiving end of my mother's glares and arm pinches during church for sliding off the pew to explore people's shoes.

After fifteen minutes had passed in the waiting room I launched myself out of the chair.

"I'll be right back," I said to the receptionist, who didn't even look up, let alone acknowledge my announcement.

To pass the time I walked to the local health food store adjacent to the clinic, where Jacob had bagged groceries as a teen one summer. I ambled past a mound of organic cantaloupes in a sidewalk bin, fondling a few of them before wandering inside the store. Within minutes I found myself at the massage supplies section where I sometimes filled my blue bottles with grapeseed oil. I paused at the aromatherapy shelf and snorted a few whiffs of lavender and chamomile in an effort to calm my nerves prior to the dreaded pelvic exam.

I thought about buying some veggies before leaving except that I'd walked from home without my back-pack. I could probably carry the bag but knowing I had a couple massage clients later that afternoon, I didn't want to wear out my arms. When a friend had once questioned my son about whether people still asked to have their groceries carried to the car, he'd answered, "Only the skinny, tired vegans." I was neither skinny nor vegan but suddenly felt like a wuss for not wanting to carry a bag a mere eight blocks back home.

It ended up being ninety minutes before a woman with painted-on eyebrows and brown-lined lips ushered me back to the examining room and instructed me to don the paper gown. I knew the routine and I knew she knew I knew the routine but I pretended to listen, much like I do when flight attendants go over their safety demonstrations. I don't like thinking about speculums any more than I like thinking about crashing in an airplane.

It wasn't until I climbed on the table and looked up at the charts on the wall that I remembered the last time I'd been in this room. A few years earlier Jacob had contracted a painful ear infection so I'd trotted him down to the same health clinic. Unfortunately the only available space was the gyno-room and when I tracked him down after filling out paperwork at the front counter I'd found him wide-eyed, surrounded by cross-sectioned vaginas, diagrammed penises, and godforsaken photographs of horrible venereal diseases in various stages of progression. Adding to his horror were the speculum and swabs neatly laid out on the counter.

"You need to move to the table so the doctor can examine you," I'd said.

He pointed to the stirrups with knitted socks dangling from the ends.

"I'm not sitting there. I know what happens on that table."

"They change the sheeting between patients, ya big dummy."

He stayed fastened to the doctor's stool.

"I don't care. I'm not going to sit there."

When the doctor finally entered she poked a penlight into his ears and *tsked*.

"You put any bubbles in your bath?"

Jacob nodded. He loves bubble baths.

"You know," she said, "The ear canal isn't all that unlike the vaginal canal."

He physically jerked, made a face at me that said, *she did not just compare part of my face to a woman's genitalia* and promptly pulled his head away from the doctor.

"It's true," she continued. "Lots of girls get infections from soaps, perfumes, bubbles, bath salts, etc. It messes up the Ph balance."

When she'd finished up her exam my traumatized son and I left with a prescription for an antibiotic and a proclamation from him that I was never, ever, to make an appointment at this clinic for him again.

My nurse-practitioner turned out to be gentler than most. She was a big gal with small hands and for that I was grateful but she didn't hold back when scolding me for my lack of regular check-ups.

"You need an annual exam," she said, "Not every five years."

"I know," I said. "But they hurt."

"You know what hurts? Cancer, that's what."

Ouch.

"I'm sorry. I get it, I really do."

As if to prove to her that I wasn't a wimp, as soon as she finished the exam I walked back over to the store and filled two bags with food before trudging the half mile home with my heavy load.

***

I'd not had much contact with Alice since her hospital had chosen a coworker as her donor. I'd often checked on her *Caring Bridge* page—a website for friends and families of those undergoing a health event— to follow her progress. Reading through her journal, it appeared as though she was really struggling to get her health back post-transplant. I couldn't help but wonder if they'd chosen the wrong kidney or if Alice would have responded similarly to mine. I left a note of encouragement on the website to let her know I was thinking of her and that I was scheduled for my donation in just a few short weeks.

I didn't expect to hear from her but Alice wrote back to say that she was rooting for me and for my anonymous recipient. She thanked me again for having offered to donate to her. She also asked if I'd like to communicate with her donor, Leah*, in case I had any questions or concerns about what to expect. I responded that I'd be absolutely thrilled to speak with her donor if she was willing.

A couple days later Leah called me at home.

"So, how painful was it?" I asked after thanking her for contacting me.

"I won't say it was painless but they give you meds to keep it under control. Good ones," she added, laughing.

"And you're back to work?"

"No. I'm one of the lucky ones. I have family helping me and I'm fortunate to work in the same office as Alice, so the staff was very generous about giving me as much time off as I wanted. I decided I'd rather wait until I'm fully recovered before going back to a full work schedule."

"How long will that be?"

"A couple of months, probably."

I knew there was no way I could take a couple of months off work so I probed a little further.

"But you felt okay after a month, right?"

"I felt pretty good by then, yes. A little tired. It takes a while for the anesthesia to completely leave your system."

"Was there anything you didn't expect? Any surprises?"

"Not really. Oh wait. Right before surgery I got really anxious. I thought I'd totally thought everything through and suddenly I was like, *I could die!* It wasn't a full blown panic attack but I remember feeling really scared."

"So how did you get through it?"

"My family reminded me I could back out if I wanted to. For some reason that took the pressure off and I calmed down pretty quickly."

"Would you do it again?"

This time she didn't hesitate.

"Absolutely."

"Thanks so much for talking with me about it Leah. I really appreciate it."

"No problem, Ellie. Please call any time if you have other questions."

Of course as soon as we hung up I had more questions. Like *does it feel any different walking around with one kidney?* I'd already been told that a kidney is about the size of a small fist and weighs only a quarter of a pound so I doubted that I'd miss the weight of my organ. But I wondered if she ate differently, drank more water, or had to pee more or less frequently. On a more emotional level I wanted to know how she'd feel if the kidney failed to thrive in Alice. The circumstances for Leah were different because she was friends with the recipient but when Kathy and I were waiting for a matched pair I'd had similar thoughts. I'd been so afraid of failing her. Not knowing my recipient was starting to look more and more like a blessing.

I thought about emailing Leah but she seemed like a rather private person and I didn't want her experience to influence my optimism about the upcoming transplant. The owner and lead instructor at the massage school I'd attended in Kalamazoo used to tell her students, "Fear is just excitement wearing other clothes," meaning that our attitude is what frames our expectations. I decided to dress my questions up in rose-colored glasses and start focusing as much as possible on positive outcomes.

FIFTEEN

December 2010

My client Rich always brings his little white dog to his monthly massage treatments. Charlie starts out on the sofa but nearly always ends up leaping onto the massage table to join his owner. As usual the dog had planted himself on top of the sheet.

"What's a Medical Directive?" I asked, moving Charlie to uncover Rich's left leg.

"It's a document listing your wishes in the event you're unable to make decisions for yourself. You really ought to have one before major surgery. I'd be happy to draw it up for you."

A few days later I met Rich in his law office to sign the papers. He'd asked in advance for a list of the people I'd want called in the event their services were needed.

"You mean like if I were in a coma or something?"

"Exactly," Rich said, "starting with the person who would be most able to make a prompt decision during a difficult or emotional situation."

This was an easy choice. My friend Mark is the most pragmatic person I've ever known. We met shortly before Jacob left for boarding school in the ninth grade. Over time we realized that although we liked each other's company, enjoyed working on home projects together, and made great snuggling companions, we were not "couple" material. In fact we're so different from each other in terms of our belief systems and general outlook it's amazing we got together in the first place. I'm a wise-cracking, happy-go-lucky, laid back, urban hippie who dies her hair pink and glues flowers to her shoes (when I wear them). Mark, on the other hand, is a self-described nerdy, somewhat-cynical hermit who can't dance and counts beans for a living. Mark also happens to be a loyal, highly-intelligent, generous man. Although we didn't have chemistry in the romantic sense we had *something*. I don't know what to call it other than the old opposites-attract kind of thing. Mark brought a sense of stability and order to my messy life and I stirred up his somewhat mundane existence with what he described as "quirkiness."

Not all my quirks are good ones. Mark graciously tolerated my forgetfulness, forgave my perpetual tardiness, and was infinitely patient with my impulsiveness, which says a lot about someone who likes order in his life. Mark is also a person who rarely says, "I love you." He doesn't have to because his actions speak for him. If I needed help with a project around the house he'd show up. If he sensed I was short for a mortgage payment he'd hide money in my purse or tuck a check in the mail. And if I needed to talk he'd listen for hours without my ever feeling judged, even when I deserved it.

Until our mutual decision to end the romantic aspect of our friendship, Mark and I shared satisfying rituals that included glorious foot rubs, morning coffee, and solving the Sunday crossword. Mark once said, "There is no such thing as relationship, there is only relating. Once you turn it into a ship all your energy goes into keeping it afloat." I don't know if he came up with that himself but it remains one of my favorite truisms.

Our friendship is by far one of the most generous and lasting I've ever experienced. In addition to naming him on my medical directive he was also the person I'd elected to accompany me on the day of surgery.

When a friend asked why I would choose Mark over a girlfriend or my son, I said, "Because he's a project manager and he's used to problem solving."

What I didn't say was that in addition to being a dear friend, I think he sees me as one of his most beloved and challenging projects. When I asked him if he'd be my medical advocate before, during, and after the surgery he didn't hesitate before agreeing.

"Of course," he'd said.

And that was that.

Rich was the one who had asserted my need for a medical directive but it was Mark who insisted I compose a will.

"If I'm going to be your plug-puller I need to know your wishes." He'd said it matter-of-factly, like he says most things.

A week before surgery I found a yellow legal pad and carried it to the swivel rocker known in my family as *the hundred dollar chair*. I leaned back, closed my eyes, and thought about what I needed to write. Creaky groans punctuated the quiet as I churned back and forth. The rhythm is familiar, like the lullaby cadence of backseat naps on lazy childhood trips to visit relatives. Trips that sometimes included the original owner of this particular chair.

It came from my grandfather who bought it when he and my grandmother resided at Spring Port Trailer Court in Fruitport, Michigan. The details of my grandfather's purchase are a little fuzzy but what I do remember is that one day he went out and bought a brown velveteen swivel rocker and he paid a whopping hundred dollars for it. As with most depression-era grandparents a hundred bucks was a hefty wad of cash. Knowing my grandfather he probably got the chair marked-down. This phrase would be certain to set a row of perm-rodded heads nodding in reverent appreciation when my grandmother would later shout the story from under her plastic hood in the Busy Bee Beauty Shoppe.

My genes are rooted in thriftiness inherited from a family who never pays full price for anything. I can still recall how joyous my mother would react upon finding a sale-priced dress she could get zipped despite her bountiful hips testing the strength of the seams.

"Look at the tag," she'd say, backing up to her younger sister. "Size *eight*."

Not to be outdone, my Aunt Ginny would pull off her shoe and shove it in my mother's face.

"Size 9 1/2. *Narrow*." (Dutch girls are known for their big feet, something even wooden clogs can't hide.) And then in the ultimate slam dunk she'd add, "On sale. *$2.99.*"

Unable to conceal her awe my mother would gasp in admiration, the extra breath being all it took to pop the button on the waist of her too-small dress.

The problem with this mode of thinking is that sometimes my mother would return from shopping with a pair of shiny patent leather ill-fitting shoes.

"Look!" she'd exclaim. "Only a dollar-ninety-five!"

To which my sister would shake her head.

"But Mom, they're not your size."

It didn't matter. A bargain was a bargain and she'd make like Prince Charming until she found a pair of grateful feet for those shoes, usually one of us. For the next year, one unlucky daughter would end up with toilet paper crammed into the toe of her new shoes to keep them from falling off.

Years later when my grandmother died and my grandfather moved in with my parents, the hundred dollar chair moved in with him. A dozen years later I sat in it as my mother took her last painful breath before leaving this world. I rocked in it for a long while, watching her cancer-wracked body transform into a hollow shell. When the undertaker finally carried my mother past us and out of the house, I thought about how life passes through rather than by us.

As I sat in the hundred dollar chair writing my will, I could almost see my grandfather's crinkly hands absentmindedly stroking the velvet with his thumb as he rocked away his afternoons. After we cleaned out my mother's house and sold off most of the contents, the chair ended up in my living room. A decade later it followed me to California. The velvet has long since rubbed off the arms and there's a tear in the seat cushion but it still brings me comfort when I sit in it. Someday the chair may outlive its use but you couldn't give me a hundred bucks for it now. Hell, you're lucky if I even let you sit in it.

I stared at the messy words on the lined yellow pages in my lap, many of them scratched out and replaced. *How does one choose who gets what, when most of what you cherish isn't tangible?* I spent the next several hours cobbling together several pages of sentimental dispensation telling my children how much I loved them and my grandchildren how sorry I was for not being more present in their lives. The more I wrote the more I felt I needed to say, and the more melancholy I became. By the time I finished I was exhausted and crawled into bed as soon as the sun set behind the fog bank that crawled into SLO from the west.

Insomnia struck for the third night in a row as I woke in a puddle of perspiration a couple of hours later. Mother Nature has a wicked sense of humor. I'd moved to California when I was thirty-nine in order to escape the blustery cold winters and long months of chill that froze me to the bone, year after year. Three short months of a Michigan summer was never long enough to completely warm my body fully before the dark clouds of October drew an icy arm around us, occasionally burying jack-o-lanterns in a foot of snow. It took seven coastal winters for me to completely thaw out.

Up until my late forties I'd basked in the glow of this sunny state with no seeming limit to my enjoyment of even the hottest days. One day everything changed. Somewhere in the middle of my back a fire started. It crept up my spine and flushed my cheeks with a prickly heat that sent me to the nearest open window. At least three fans oscillated from the coolest corners of my studio on any given day. Sometimes I'd pause to pull my sundress over the box fan, creating a cool tent for my sweaty legs as I basked in the comfort of my own private breeze, deliriously content for a few precious moments between hot flashes. And yet still I'd awaken during the night with my comforter kicked off the bed, drowning in soaked covers, my skin against the sheet like gum on a hot sidewalk.

It wasn't just hot sweats. Menopause began wreaking havoc in all sorts of odd and frustrating manners. I could no longer read printed materials without magnifying glasses. My hair grew thinner and my waist did just the opposite. Within two years I went from a loose size eight to a snug size ten. With no change in diet or exercise I gained twenty pounds as a circus of hormones turned my body into a big top of unrelenting surprises. I also found myself forgetting stuff, something one of my menopausal friends calls *the stupids*. I did my best to go with the flow but the night sweats were the worst.

As I surfed yet another hot flash while browsing the web on my laptop in bed, I recalled the thermostat wars of my childhood. My dad, wearing a sweater over his white shirt and long johns under polyester slacks, would sidle over to the living room wall and twist the dial until the familiar whoomph of the gas-ignited flames kicked in. My sisters and I would dive for nearby floor registers, anxiously awaiting the hot dusty breath as our old furnace wheezed from a dark corner in the basement. Huddled over a metal grate behind the bathroom door I'd bask in the glow of my own private hearth, deliriously content. Until Mom appeared from out of the kitchen where she'd been slaving over our dinner and abruptly turned the thermostat down.

Eventually my father would grow cold and turn it up again, and the whole thing started over as they battled over room temperature in a silly game of furnace tag. My parents' Sunday afternoon ritual lasted almost into my teens, even after we moved out of the old two-story parsonage and into a house with a more efficient furnace and better insulation. By then some of the house rules had relaxed and I was allowed to change into slacks after church but winter was winter and Dad's blood still ran thin. I continued to enjoy sitting by the register reading the Sunday comics, sometimes falling asleep curled next to the vent with a blanket and a pillow.

One day smack dab in the middle of a glorious furnace-induced nap, Mom marched across the living room and twisted the thermostat all the way off. Not down. *Off.* With sweat beading between her furrowed brows she crossed her arms, daring my father to eject himself from his Easy-Boy and challenge her. He took one look at his flushed wife and grabbed an afghan off the back of the chair. Victorious, she strode back to the kitchen. As soon as she was out of sight my dad tip-toed over to the thermostat and notched it back up.

A few minutes later Mom stomped back into the room and turned it down so forcefully the lid popped off. Dad leapt to his feet and snapped the cover back in place before turning it up. She opened a window. He closed it. She opened two more. He closed and locked them. From opposite sides of the living room they stared each other down without saying a word. Ours was a fundamentalist Christian home where swearing wasn't allowed, but if looks were cuss words they were both damned to hell for sure.

In that instant my mother smiled the kind of smile where one corner of the mouth tilts toward lunacy. Without taking her eyes off my dad, she stripped down to her bra and panties then walked past her stunned husband and opened the front door facing our neighbor's house. I looked at my dad, wondering how he'd handle my obviously unhinged mom without causing a stir, another thing we Midwesterners weren't supposed to do. In a house where he was outnumbered by women six to one, he ran his household with a firm but loving omnipotence, reserving the occasional fits of rage for only the direst of circumstances.

I figured this was one of those times. I was just about to slink down the hall to my bedroom when he answered my gaze with a shrug. For the first time in my life she had beaten him. I watched in amazement as he slowly walked over to my mother and gently kissed her on the back of her wet neck before quietly closing the front door. Mom put her clothes back on and Dad put on another sweater. From then on the thermostat remained at sixty-five degrees.

The earlier memory of my grandfather and his beloved chair, and now thinking about my mom and dad, left me feeling lonely and maudlin. I set my laptop on the floor by my bed, too tired to return it to the desk, knowing full well the odds against my remembering it was there when I'd step out of bed the next morning. I nudged Bella, who'd sneaked up when I wasn't paying attention. Instead of kicking her off the bed I gently edged her over so we both fit. Propping my glasses on the night stand, I turned off the light and faced the fan, letting the wind dry my wet face and hoping the motor would hum me into peaceful oblivion.

SIXTEEN

December 2010 (Continued)

On the day before surgery, I woke at five and did what everyone says you're not supposed to do if you want to get back to sleep; I lifted my laptop back onto the bed and started charting Amtrak routes to San Francisco. I love trains and was actually looking forward to the time the trip would give me to relax and meditate on the way to the hospital. But when I plugged in the route I discovered the train wouldn't get me to the Bay Area in time for my scheduled lab work. I couldn't take my car because I'd be unable to drive for several weeks after surgery. My friend Danielle had previously offered to take me so I emailed her with my predicament and asked if the offer still stood.

Danielle is the kind of person most people in the Midwest think of when they imagine Californians. Between her flowing dresses and sun-kissed cheeks she is the epitome of the Goddess archetype and not the least bit hesitant to own it. Her waist-length brown hair is usually adorned with flowers or feathers (or both) and she wears healing stones around her neck. Her infectious chortle is so joyful I half expect to see rainbows stream from her mouth when she laughs.

I love Danielle. Although her beliefs tend toward the far end of the New Age spectrum I respect the differences in our methods. She looks deep into your eyes when she's listening, a rare trait in most people. Like me she's a massage therapist but she mostly prefers energy work to performing more clinical bodywork. Her walls are decorated with chakra posters rather than muscle charts and she experiments with sound therapy using tuning forks as well as crystals and other various mystical modalities.

Danielle had recently spent a year traveling around New Zealand in an old station wagon. When she returned to the states I'd let her sleep in my camper for several months while she looked for a permanent place. She eventually found the perfect home in downtown SLO then promptly split to Hawaii for the winter. Danielle was back in SLO again and had recently purchased a VW van complete with dyed curtains and a bed in the back for spontaneous road trips.

Let me know if the offer to take me to the hospital still stands, I wrote. *It would be fun to ride up to the Bay Area together.*

I gave up on going back to sleep and spent the rest of the morning deciding what to pack for one night at the hotel and three to five days in the hospital. After much inner-kvetching I finally narrowed it down to a pair of comfy yoga pants, tank top, sweatshirt, warm jacket, knit cap, and a pair of hand-made wool socks that my friend Dominique had sent from Northern India. She'd been teaching English to Tibetan refugees since moving out of our granny unit. The package had arrived a few days before in an odd-shaped linen lump sealed with wax and tied with string. When I brought it to my nose it smelled exotic, like a world I didn't know and yet found vaguely familiar. After carefully untying the string I lifted each thing to my nose. First the brightly colored wool blanket that would be perfect for my massage table, then the handmade socks, and finally the beads that had been blessed by His Holiness The Dali Lama and which I immediately looped over my left wrist.

I'd saved her hand-written letter for last. Getting an old-fashioned letter via snail mail is an extraordinary gift. Unlike hastily-written emails or shorthand text messages, a handwritten letter demands more from the receiver. I'd made a cup of coffee and sat in the hundred dollar chair to read Dominique's sad tales of Tibetan refugees. I traced the words with my finger on the paper as I read. Although happy for her newfound love of volunteerism, I missed my dear, dear friend. Her missive was interspersed with funny stories about her students and the one-eyed monkey that visited her window each day. She described bathing in ice-cold water when the heaters intermittently stopped working and the time she nearly barfed after tasting Yak cheese offered by a well-meaning Tibetan.

Dominique is another example of the type of person Midwesterners likely imagine when they think of Left-Coasters. Our friendship began the day I'd run an ad for the granny unit after the most recent tenant had given notice. Most of the folks who responded to the ad weren't a good fit. The first applicant reeked of cigarettes despite insisting she was a non-smoker and another had three cats. Yet another wanted to know if it would be okay to practice his drums while living next door. To a massage therapist. Um, *no*.

I don't normally subscribe to hooky-do mystical stuff but when Dominique walked up the driveway there was something about her that was different. The only way I can describe it is that she had an aura about her that made me immediately feel at ease. She wore a white blouse over jeans and hiking shoes on her feet. Her silver hair defied a youthful face with deep, hooded eyes and blushing high cheekbones.

"Hello Eldonn-*a*," she said in her French accent, putting emphasis on the last syllable of my name. "Thank you for letting me see your place."

"Of course," I said, having already pictured her as the perfect, middle aged, non-partying, responsible tenant I'd hoped to find.

"What do you think?" I asked.

She smiled as she looked around the studio.

"It's pair*fect!*"

"Wonderful. Because you seem perfect," I said, doing my best not to unconsciously imitate her as I have a habit of embarrassingly doing.

She turned toward me and frowned like a pouting child.

"You might not think so after I tell you…" She trailed off.

"What is it?"

"Better to show you," she said, motioning me to follow her to the Jeep parked at the curb. It instantly started rocking before we'd reached it. "Maple!" she shouted, then turning to me, "She gets excited around new people."

It was then that I spotted the source of the rocking Jeep. A huge, full-grown Rottweiler barked once then panted as we approached.

"Oh," I said. "Oh my."

"You see?" Again with the adorable pout. "I don't blame you. She's a big dog. But she is very sweet and I won't part with her even though everyone says no."

I carefully approached the car window and lifted the back of my hand toward Maple's nose. She took a sniff then instantly enveloped my entire hand up to the wrist, mouthing it gently.

"Maple, let go! No!" said her owner. "I'm sorry. But that's what Rotties do. It's their way of accepting you into the pack." Dominique patted her beloved dog's head. "She's traveled with me for a year and it's time for us to settle down but it's been difficult to find a place."

"Well," I said, "I believe you just found one."

"Really?"

"Really. Welcome to the urban oasis!"

I'd half expected Dominique to mouth my hand but we hugged instead, which is what people do when they accept each other into their pack.

Standing in the room where Dominique once lived I gathered my things for the trip to the hospital in San

Francisco. I carefully folded Dominique's letter and tucked it into my duffle bag to read again at the hospital. Before zipping up the top I added my little statuette of K'Wan Yin, a gift from Nick. Although I'm not a practicing Buddhist I've grown fond of this little bodhisattva of compassion. At the last minute I grabbed my father's well worn Bible from the bookshelf, fanning through pages of scribbled notes and highlighted scripture before sliding it into the front pocket of my bag. I'm not a practicing Christian either but decided it couldn't hurt to take all the blessings I could get.

***

Danielle was running late, which is not unusual for Danielle, but we hadn't allowed a lot of leeway for possible traffic so I was starting to worry just a little. When the phone rang and her name popped up I was relieved until she spoke.

"Hey, I'm having some trouble with the van."

I felt my neck muscles tighten at the prospect of being late for my lab appointments. I was accustomed to being on "Danielle Time" when waiting for my friend but this wasn't a coffee or beach date. There were lots of people downstream counting on me.

"Hmmm," I said. "Bill offered to drive if I needed a ride. I could call him."

"Your ex? How about you just meet me at my mechanic's and we'll take your car?"

I took a deep breath.

"I suppose that might work. How would I get my car back home?"

"I'll drive it back to SLO. I can hang with you in the city overnight and drive home after your surgery on Thursday."

"Okay," I said. "I'll meet you in ten minutes."

Half an hour later Danielle pulled up and waved as she ran inside the garage to give the mechanic her keys.

"Sorry I'm late," she said, when she climbed into the

passenger seat. She stroked her miniature Australian shepherd as he panted in her lap. "I had to pick my little guy up from the groomers."

"No problem," I said. "But we better get going."

I pointed my car back toward the highway while Danielle typed the address of the hotel into the navigation ap on her phone. We weren't even a quarter of the way up the Highway 101 grade when a red light blinked at me from the dashboard.

"Shit!" I said. "My idiot light just came on."

Danielle leaned in to look at the glowing light. "It's probably just low on oil. Or maybe water."

I felt myself start to hyperventilate. Danielle reached over and patted my knee.

"Calm down, Ellie. It'll be okay. We'll get there."

I took some more deep breaths, hoping my pulse would stop hip-hopping in my chest. I kept looking at the light, trying to figure out if it was the engine warning or the radiator level as we started up the steep grade northward. When we reached a turnoff I pulled over.

"I can't do this, Danielle. I'm sorry. I just can't take a chance. I'm going to call Bill and see if he's still available."

I phoned my wasband, as I liked to call him, and he picked up on the second ring.

"Hey, I know I said I wouldn't' need you to drive me to San Francisco but I'm having car problems. Is there any chance you could still take me?"

"I'll be there as soon as I can," he said.

"I'm sorry to be such a pain in the ass."

"Don't worry about it. I can be at your house within twenty minutes."

As we drove back down the grade, Danielle kept apologizing.

"I feel like such a failure as your friend. I'm sorry I've let you down."

"Hey," I said, grabbing her ring-studded hand. "You

didn't let me down. Just the fact that you were willing to do this means a lot. I think it just wasn't meant to be."

"Maybe Mercury is in retrograde. You know, all these mechanical problems, it sounds like a planetary disturbance."

"Maybe," I said. "But I think we just both have old sucky cars.

She laughed, throwing her head back in the way she always does, filling the air between us with unbridled glee. I couldn't help but laugh with her.

"I love you, Ellie," she said when I pulled up in front of my house. "I'll be holding you in the light."

"Thank you Danielle. That means a lot to me." We shared a three-breath hug standing outside my car. "You sure you can get a ride home?"

"Don't worry about me. I'll just go say hi to my old roomies while I'm waiting for a lift."

She'd barely made it inside the house before I heard her laugh cascade down the driveway from an open window as she greeted her former housemates. I was still smiling when Bill pulled up in his Subaru Wagon.

"Hey, I'll just grab my bag out of the Beetle," I said.

Bill opened the back hatch and I tossed my duffle inside. He lowered his long legs into the driver's seat and closed the door as I hopped in the other side. He glanced at me before putting the car into gear.

"Ready?"

"I've been ready for over an hour."

As he pulled onto the northbound lanes of the highway I studied the gauges illuminating his dashboard. Knowing Bill, the oil had been changed, tire pressure checked, and scheduled maintenance completed well before the prescribed date. I settled back into the comfortable seat and sighed.

'You okay?" he asked.

"Yeah. I'm okay."

"You sure?"

I looked over at his hands, steady on the wheel at ten and

two.

"Yeah," I said. "Really sure."

***

About an hour south of San Francisco it started. Not just raining. Pouring. Sheets of water hit the windshield as the sky darkened under the heavy clouds. Bill adjusted his position, his mouth set in a straight line.

I leaned forward.

"Kind of hard to see I bet. I didn't even think to check the weather."

"Driving in the rain isn't a problem. My full bladder, however, is."

We'd made a gas, bathroom and sandwich stop back in Soledad, the halfway mark for motorists traveling between SLO and the Bay Area. But he obviously needed another.

"Can you make it or shall we find a bathroom?"

"I hate to get off the freeway when I'm not familiar with the route and the best place to get back on."

I sucked the last bit of water from my soda cup and tilted it toward him.

"We could probably pull over there where's there's a wide shoulder," I said, pointing.

Funny how once you've lived with somebody, spent years sleeping next to them, shared countless outdoor hikes where peeing in the wild is second nature, suddenly one of you is feeling shy. Particularly the one who has to pee in a cup while the other is sitting next to you.

"Don't look," he kidded, filling first his then my fountain cup. He opened the door to quickly dump them but the rain still managed to soak his arms. I waited as he disinfected his hands with wet-wipes from the glove compartment before merging back onto the highway.

"Don't tell anyone about this," he said.

"Oh, I won't," I lied.

It was after eight by the time we arrived at the Kabuki, a hotel in San Francisco's Japantown, less than eight blocks from CPMC. I offered to let Bill spend the night in what was to have been Danielle's bed, knowing how difficult it would be to turn around and drive the four hours back to SLO in the rain.

He pulled my bag from the back of his car.

"I think I'll head back. Taking your ex-wife to San Francisco is one thing. Staying overnight with her might be a lot to ask of a girlfriend."

"Okay, I just wanted to offer." We hugged before he climbed back into the car. "Thank you again for everything. I owe you."

"You don't owe me anything, I was glad to help. It's the least I can do under the circumstances."

I pushed his door closed and waited while he fastened the seat belt. "Drive safely," I shouted, as he waved and pulled away.

Standing in the glow of the hotel street lamps I watched his taillights disappear around the corner. I thought about his current girlfriend, having known firsthand what it was like to be with a man who successfully sustains lasting friendships with many of the women he has dated or married. I'd met Patricia a few summers earlier during one of SLO's downtown concert series. She and Bill were there along with his second wife Laurel, who was visiting from Michigan and staying with Bill.

The four of us leaned against the mission wall laughing and swaying to the music together that evening. I wondered then how this man had been blessed with three fabulous women who loved him and who were also loving toward each other. What I now understand is that it wasn't so much about him as the strong compassionate women he chose.

After the concert we'd walked to a nearby Mexican restaurant for dinner.

When the waiter stopped by I said, "I'll have the chicken

fajitas, blue cheese on my salad, and by the way all three of us have seen this guy naked."

Actually I only thought the last part of that statement but I did have the chicken fajitas. I doubt I was the only one thinking about each other's various entwined anatomies, especially Bill, who was crammed into a booth with one present and two former lovers. If I were a guy I'd probably have stood on the table, pounded my chest, and grunted enthusiastically.

As it turned out all three women were in varying stages of menopause and found common ground as more than just present or former first ladies of my ex. We traded hot flash and crying jag stories while mostly ignoring Bill, who seemed happy just to be included in our giddy girlishness. Although he probably wished we'd shut up about menopause and spontaneously suggest we have a 4-way.

On our way back to the car Laurel and I followed behind Bill and Patricia like a pair of rehearsed flower girls. I'd seen the two of them together on several occasions but that night was the first time I'd really felt their love for each other. I understood then that it's possible to love a person deeply enough to wish for his happiness more than wanting yourself to be part of it. In the midst of this realization I'd whispered to Laurel that I was glad Bill had found Patricia because she's been really good for him.

"Yes, she is," Laurel said. She squeezed my hand and grinned. "But then we *all* have."

"Are you a guest, Ma'am?"

"What?"

A uniformed bellhop extended his hand to take my bag.

"Welcome to the Kabuki," he said.

"Oh, yes. I mean yes, I'm a guest but I've got it, thanks." I said, and scrambled through the front doors into the hotel lobby.

Because we'd reserved a pet-friendly room for Danielle's dog I found myself sitting on one bed then the other, and back to the first one again, hoping to find a tolerable distance from the undercurrent of animal urine. Midwesterner's are not complainers. We rarely make a fuss or send a steak back. But understanding the importance of a good night's sleep before the big day ahead, I broke with ancestral protocol and rode the elevator back down to the front desk. Fortunately, the clerk was very accommodating.

"No problem," she said, handing me a new key. "Enjoy your stay."

The second room was the antithesis of the first. It was almost as if the Kabuki had stitched together two completely different hotels with one side being an aging, smelly motel and the other a luxury destination. Painted rice paper doors slid apart on soundless runners to expose a view of the city. The beds sat high with crisp white sheets turned down over gorgeous duvets and the bathroom boasted a Japanese-style tub that was almost as deep as it was long.

I immediately filled the tub as hot as I could stand it before immersing myself in the steaming water, adding more as it cooled. When I finally emerged an hour later, I slipped into the provided kimono and propped myself on firm pillows in the bed. I pulled the legal pad from my pack and tore off several tortuous pages, wadded them into a ball, and tossed it toward the wastebasket, missing by a couple of feet. I clicked the pen top and began again.

This is my last will and testament. Being of sound mind and body I hereby ask that my children dispose of my estate in the following manner: Sell the house. Divide the proceeds amongst the three of you after paying off my debts. Give the hundred dollar chair to Jacob (he asked). Take anything of meaning to you and donate the rest to the local women's shelter or other worthy non-profit. I ask that you put my beloved dog Bella in my eldest grandaughter's care.

I made a list of people and corporations I owed,

including a few that I owed no actual money but felt a debt to for their part in making my life a better one through the generosity of their friendship. I scribbled the date and my signature at the bottom—all that's required for a legal holographic will in California—and tucked both sheets of paper into a Hotel Kabuki envelope. I wrote *Last Will and Testament* on the front and slipped it into my purse before falling into a deep sleep.

SEVENTEEN

December 15, 2010

I woke to the sounds of *Maxwell's Silver Hammer* and struggled to orient myself as I shut off my cell phone alarm. And then I did what I've done ever since menopause stole half my short-term memory cells. I silently asked myself, *Where am I? What day is it? Where do I need to be?*

The answers appeared out of order. I have lab tests this morning. I'm at the hotel. I think it's Wednesday.

The day's itinerary, printed on a sheet of CPMC letterhead that I'd left on the nightstand, affirmed my foggy brain:

Pre-Op Day (Wednesday, December 15, 2010
8:30 a.m. Preregistration & Learning Center for labs/EKG
10:00 a.m. Chest X-Ray (Hospital Radiology Dept. 2nd floor)
11:00 a.m. Pharmacy Consult (Dept of Transplant 4th floor)
11:30 a.m. Meet with Case Worker
12:30 LUNCH
2:00 p.m. Pre-Op eval with Transplant Nephrologist
3:00 p.m. Pre-Op eval with Transplant Surgeon
4:00 p.m. Pre-Op with Transplant Coordinator

A long day laid ahead, especially the part where I couldn't have coffee before blood draws and an EKG. Enjoying the luxury of a third-wave coffee shop situated right below the spa where I worked had turned me into an espresso snob. I can go without a meal but I'd already mapped out the highest-rated coffee places closest to the hospital. I planned to make a beeline for one of them the minute the last EKG wire was unsnapped from my body.

After taking the shuttle to the lab I filled out a stack of forms and waited for my name to be called. I'd expected a bunch of grumpy morning people like my coffee-deprived self but the receptionist nearly fell over himself with good cheer when I returned the forms to the front counter.

"We'll be right with you!" he said.

I'd hardly settled back into the chair when the phlebotomist showed up.

"Eldonna?"

I stared at her white, nearly perfect teeth situated between gorgeous smiling lips, then down to the clipboard in her arms.

"Eldonna?" she asked again.

"Right here," I said, standing.

"Hi! Follow me!"

I followed her. We traveled down a hallway to a row of booths where Miss Congeniality snapped a rubber strap onto my upper arm and set a small red ball into my hand.

"Okay, squeeze!"

I squeezed.

"Perfect!" She plunged a needle painlessly into my vein and untied the rubber band. "Nice veins!" she said, as she filled several vials.

"Aw shucks, these old things?"

She laughed.

"You funny!"

"I'm funnier with coffee."

"Coffee not good for you," she said, tsking.

"You might not say that if you see me in a couple of hours without it."

"Tea better for you."

"Probably. But so is sushi and I don't like that either."

Her smile disappeared and she looked at me as if I'd just cursed at a group of toddlers.

"I told you I'm funnier with coffee," I said.

She laughed but I knew it was her pretend laugh because I'd already heard the real one, the one that sounded like bells.

I rolled my sleeve back down to my wrist. ""Thank you. You're very gentle."

She patted my back before grabbing another clipboard and striding to the lobby area ahead of me, gleefully calling out the next name.

The receptionist motioned me to the front desk and handed me a card.

"Here's where you need to be next. Take the elevator up to the second floor, follow the signs."

"Thanks," I said, then added, "So is there some kind of contest going on, or are you folks always this pleasant?"

"Not a contest," he said, smiling, "but we do try to make patients feel welcome."

I shifted my purse to my other shoulder.

"You're doing an excellent job."

"Thank you. It's nice of you to say so."

I left the lab feeling buoyed by positive energy in a place one does not expect to be uplifting. At the elevators I waited three turns for other, obviously sick patients to go ahead of me as they filed inside with walkers and wheelchairs. On the fourth try a towering African American man wearing pink scrubs tapped me on the shoulder.

"Here, take this one," he said, motioning to an inconspicuous set of doors behind us. He pushed a cart full of supplies inside and motioned for me to join him. "Going up?"

Once inside I realized we were on the service elevator.

"Please excuse our mess." He nodded toward the flat walls and un-tiled floor. "We're in the process of renovating."

I surveyed the scuffed cubicle and grinned.

"You should put mirrors on the walls, maybe hang a disco ball from the ceiling."

"I like that idea! And lights in the floor!"

"A virtual DJ," I added, as the doors closed.

He leaned his six-foot plus body against the back wall and grinned.

"You look more like a visitor than a patient."

"I'm not a patient. Yet. But tomorrow I'm having a nephrectomy."

"Aw, I'm sorry, girl. Wasn't my business."

"It's okay. I'm not sick. I'm a donor."

The elevator dinged and the doors opened.

"I'm Daniel," he said.

I shook his hand.

"Ellie," I said, the name I always give when I don't want to get into a spelling, pronunciation, and etymology discussion.

"Nice to meet you, Ellie."

"You, too. Thanks for the ride."

As I stepped off the elevator he reached across to hold the door open.

"What time is your surgery, Ellie? If you don't mind my asking?"

"4:00."

"Ima say a prayer for you."

"Say one for my recipient too, will you Daniel?"

"You got it." The doors closed but not before I heard a voice on the other side loudly singing, *Won't you take me to Funky Town?*

The friendliness didn't stop with the blood lab or the elevator guy. My sweet young x-ray tech, the matronly woman who ran my EKG, and the pharmacist who went over the meds I'd be given prior to, during, and after surgery, could all have been running for political office. I'd never dealt with such a genuinely friendly group of medical professionals in my life. Despite my foodless and un-caffeinated state, I left the hospital feeling better than when I'd arrived.

I set out on a mission to find a good cup of coffee. Half way up the steep six-block hill I started feeling light-headed. I leaned against an apartment building to steady myself, fearing I was about to pass out, and quickly sat down on the sidewalk. I dropped my head between my knees and waited for the blood to return to my brain. People stepped around what was probably a normal scene on their daily treks through San Francisco, which made me feel even more uncomfortable than my hypoglycemic state. *I'm okay*, I wanted to tell passersby, *I'm not indigent, I'm just feeling faint.*

As soon as I felt well enough to stand I forced myself to my feet and took a couple steps. When I pulled on my jacket a crumpled five dollar bill fell out on the sidewalk. I wracked my brain trying to remember if I'd had it in my hand when I got dizzy. I decided not to over-think whether it was mine or if some stranger had dropped it on me when my head was between my knees. I tucked the bill in my pocket and slowly climbed the rest of the way up the hill. Good coffee, after all, doesn't come cheap.

Two espressos and half a falafel sandwich later I zipped my jacket against the brisk wind and waited for the shuttle bus. Fortunately they run on the half hour and I didn't have to wait long. I climbed in and took the seat right behind the driver, a short olive-skinned man in his mid sixties. As I watched the procession of patients and medical staff climb aboard the bus I became increasingly aware of diversity rarely seen in SLO, let alone the small Michigan town where I grew up. Amidst my fellow Black, Asian, Middle-Eastern, and Hispanic riders, for once I was the minority.

The nurses and techs, dressed in scrubs or wearing hospital badges, joked with the driver and each other. They traded stories about their jobs, their children and their partners in that familiar way between people whose lives overlap on a daily basis. I listened and smiled in the manner one does when on the outside of an inside joke. We bumped along with taxis honking, sirens blaring, and more than one deranged man marching in front of the bus punching his fists at the dense air as he cursed.

Unlike most people I like busses. As a kid I used to envy the riders who boarded the big yellow bus that waited in front of our tiny school every afternoon. I thought it unfair that I had to walk to school, walk home for lunch—missing all the lunchroom fun—and walk home again at the end of every day. Busses were like forts to me, where any number of magical things happen. Like my first kiss, for example.

It was a rickety old school bus painted white, with *New Era Bible Church* printed in black letters on one side and a Bible verse—I think it was John 3:16—on the other. Every week one of the deacons or my dad would drive to the outskirts of town and round up kids from the trailer park and tract houses surrounding a tiny man-made lake that the developers had actually named Lake Tahoe. The church made it their mission to drive these poor sinners into town in hopes of saving their godforsaken souls.

Like most of the trailer park and Lake Tahoe kids, we regulars at New Era Bible Church considered Duane a fast boy in terms of life experience. When teased about his prominent nose he claimed he was part Ojibwa. He wore his brown hair long with bangs that hung over his eyes, making him have to flip his head every few seconds in order to see anything. Growing up in a rural town with a population of four hundred or so people, I'd had very little exposure to the outside world or the dens of iniquity my father constantly warned me about. But I suspected Duane had probably seen those dens. Maybe even lived in one. And at thirteen years old I was drawn to him like a raccoon to a parking lot behind Burger King.

Duane and I sat in church that muggy summer evening,

pretending to listen to my Dad preach. At some point our fingers touched and he laid his hand over mine. Every nerve on the surface of my skin danced as he lightly ran his thumb over the back of my hand. A few other nerves I hadn't been tuned into put on their dancin' shoes as well. Eventually our youth pastor caught sight of what was going on and separated us. But I could still feel his hand on mine, that tingle shooting from my fingers to places hidden beneath a hand-me-down dress and a sweat-soaked cotton slip.

After prayer meeting let out Duane smiled at me, flipped his hair and mouthed something I couldn't hear. When I didn't move he flipped it again then walked away. *Ooooh, I get it. You're flipping your hair but what you're really doing is pointing me in the direction of the flipping.* I followed him out the back door of the church where he immediately grabbed me and gave me a long, soft kiss. I kept my mouth closed but he didn't. I wanted to wipe his spit off my face but was afraid I'd offend him so I just stood there hoping it would evaporate quickly.

"I like you," he half-whispered, in his fourteen year-old croaky voice.

Well, that was enough for me.

"Me, too," I said. "I mean I like you, too."

"Why don't you ride along on the bus tonight?"

My legs were trembling in my patent leathers.

"I have to ask my dad."

He let go of my waist.

"Well, what are you waiting for?"

I ran back inside and tugged on my dad's suit coat as he stood in the back of the auditorium, shaking hands with a parishioner who ran an insurance company and owned a house with three bathrooms.

"Daddy, can I ride with you on the bus tonight?"

"Go ask your mother." It was his standard answer.

I found my mother in the church basement, washing coffee cups with one of the other ladies.

"Mom can I ride on the bus with Daddy tonight?"

"If it's okay with him it's okay with me." Her standard answer.

Several minutes later I climbed the steps behind Mr. Vandoren*, who'd offered to drive the bus so Pastor Edwards could go home to his family. Duane sat in the very back, grinning. As I approached, he patted the seat next to him on the window side. I squeezed past his legs and sat down, feeling shy and watched by all the bus kids who'd turned around to face us as they bounced in their seats.

Duane made a threatening motion with his hands and said, "Get the hell out of here."

The back half of the bus cleared out immediately. I don't know if I was more impressed by his command over the other kids or that he'd just said *hell*.

Mr. Vandoren pulled out of the parking lot and pointed the bus toward Lake Tahoe. As we rumbled along U.S. 31 Duane put his arm around me. I stared straight ahead. Determined, he turned my head with his hand and kissed me again. This time he forced his tongue through my lips and swirled it around in my mouth. I was totally disgusted and completely fascinated at the same time. My older sister had told me about french kissing but I never imagined I'd be doing it.

Again with the party in the nether-regions of my body. I felt uncomfortable. Uneasy. Something in the way he kissed me told me he'd done this a lot, probably with a lot of girls. Probably a lot more than just kissing. Maybe he'd want me to do other stuff. I wanted him to stop. I wanted to move to another seat. I wanted him to get off the bus.

Thankfully we rolled to a standstill. Mr. Vandoren turned the lights up and cranked open the front door. Duane stood and propelled his skinny body up the aisle by hoisting himself on the back of the seats then swinging his legs forward every few rows. When he got to the front of the bus, he turned, flipped his hair, and winked before chasing the younger kids up the dirt road toward their houses.

As soon as he was gone I wanted him back. I rode in silence as the bus emptied itself of the rest of the kids, my lips still numb from that boy pressing his face against mine. Finally, Mr. Vandoren pulled back into the gravel parking lot behind the church and got out, forgetting I was still on the bus. He began whistling *Surely Goodness and Mercy Shall Follow Me*, a song I used to think was about two angels named Shirley and Marcy as he walked away.

I sat alone in the dark and watched Mr. Vandoren disappear up the road with his Bible under his arm, still whistling. Across the street the second-story windows of our parsonage threw light from behind wide horizontal blinds. Bats dove for mosquitoes under the street lamp in front of our house and somewhere in the distance a coon dog howled at the end of his chain. When I finally stood, my skin unstuck itself from the vinyl bus seat, leaving an orange-peel pattern on the back of my stinging thighs. I kicked off my shoes and walked barefoot on the still-warm blacktop, daring the bats to tangle themselves in my hair as I crossed over the crumbling road of my childhood.

Back in the city a fellow shuttle-bus rider nudged me with her elbow.

"I think this is your stop."

"Oh, yeah, it is. Thanks."

I stumbled down the steps and stood in front of the familiar hospital where I'd had my first round of tests and interviews three years earlier. Before the shuttle pulled away I watched a young couple flirting in line as they boarded. He flipped his long kinky hair then ran his fingers through it like a rake through sun-bleached grass as he climbed the steps then wandered to the last seat in the back. I waited for the young woman's head to appear next to him but it never did. I suspect the trick only works on country bumpkins or naïve girls who never got to ride the bus.

EIGHTEEN

December 15, 2010 (Continued)

I sat in the hospital waiting room holding the get well card I'd brought for the transplant team to send along with my recipient's shiny new kidney. I was unsure if I wanted to include the printed "adoption" letter I'd written, so I hadn't sealed the envelope. As I waited for my name to be called I read the letter for the hundredth time.

Dear Friend:

By the time this letter reaches you I hope that you are in the midst of a positive recovery from surgery and that your new kidney is working hard to do what it's supposed to do, as it did for me for the past 51 years. I say "your" kidney because ever since I heard the transplant center had found a match I no longer felt it was my organ—more like I was just incubating it until the transfer could be made. Although I have always taken pretty good care of my body, in the month or so leading up to the surgery I've found myself very protective of your kidney. I've stayed away from sick people. I've been a more careful driver. I've eaten more vegetables and gotten more exercise and rest. In essence, I've treated my body a lot like when I was pregnant.

I decided to write you because if it were me I'd want to know a little bit about the person who raised my kidney on the first leg of its journey.

Your kidney was born in March of 1959 to a minister and his wife. She teethed on the back of a Baptist pew and although the religion itself didn't stick, many of the underlying philosophies did. Things like lovingkindness and compassion. Helping those in need. Doing the right thing when given difficult choices. Knowing we are all brothers and sisters in this world. You get the picture.

To be honest, your kidney's caretaker tended to learn lessons the hard way. She was married and divorced with two baby girls by the age of twenty. She married and divorced twice more and had another baby before deciding that she rather likes her own company and now lives happily alone. She loves her work as a massage therapist, which has contributed to her overall well-being. She lives a simple but gratifying life. All in all she's been good to your kidney.

The other question I would have if the tables were turned is why? Why would somebody donate their organ to a complete stranger? For me, this was about having the ability to do something proactive, to "be the change" as Gandhi liked to say. I am no saint sir, but I have made every effort in this life to leave it a better place and to reduce the suffering of others when I had the means and the ability to do so. Sometimes just by massaging tired feet or in this case, by donating what I have deemed was given to me as a "spare" in the event someone else needed it.

I tell you all this because I wanted you to know that your kidney was raised in a good home and comes to you not only with my blessing but my hope that it will continue to be of such good service to you as it was for me. I hope that by the time these words reach you your life has been changed in positive ways as much as mine has by this experience. I hope you are well and happy and loved. This, we all deserve.

All Best,

Eldonna (Ellie)

I folded the letter and tucked it into the card, took it out, then put it back in again before my name was finally called and the receptionist led me back to the consultation room.

Doctor Mahatny, who was assigned to perform my nephrectomy from the transplant center's pool of surgeons, walked into the room and smiled. From his doo-rag cap to his easy gait, he seemed young enough to be sharp but confident enough to instill a sense of trust in his capability. Unlike Doctor Bry, who'd sketched out the procedure on paper, Doctor Mahatny used his own body as a model when explaining what I could expect.

"We're going to make a couple of incisions about here—one for the camera and one for the laser—and another *here*, from where we'll deliver your kidney."

I followed the movement of his hands across the front belly of his blue scrubs.

"Will there be a big scar?"

"The two smaller ones will be about three centimeters and the one at your bikini line about seven. However, if we run into a problem there's a possibility we could open you up and do the surgery the old fashioned way." He drew an imaginary line from the side of his ribs to his hip bone. "If that happened you'd have a scar from here to here."

The way he described the surgery made it sound like a birth, and him the midwife. *We hope to deliver you naturally but if there's a complication we might have to do a caesarian section.*

"And you've done a few of these, right?" I said, smiling.

"Quite a few. The head of the nephrology department, Dr. Bry, will be assisting. You've met him, right?"

"Yes, in my initial consultation. That's awesome that you'll be working together."

"He's very good." Dr. Mahatny rose and shook my hand. "It was a pleasure to meet you, Eldonna. I'll send in Dr. Yu, your assigned nephrologist. See you tomorrow, okay?"

Had we been in Michigan I'd have answered, "Good Lord willin' and the creek don't rise!" But we were not in

Michigan and I doubt this young man had heard the idiom. Maybe even change his mind about my mental state.

"See you tomorrow!" I said, a little too enthusiastically.

Reaching the age where doctors and teachers are younger than you can be a little disconcerting. Dr. Mahatny was certainly under thirty-five. Upon first meeting my assigned nephrologist Dr. Yu, I immediately estimated him to be younger than my oldest daughter. His small frame and youthful face combined with a boyish lilt in his voice as he went over my medical history only added to the validity of my estimation.

"This is exciting for us," he said, as he moved behind a huge desk that dwarfed us both.

"It's exciting for me, too," I said. "I've been waiting a long time for this day to arrive."

"Everything looks good from our end. Your tests came out excellent and you appear very healthy."

If my mother had said this I'd have immediately thought she was referring to the extra pounds I'd put on with menopause. Somehow hearing it from a doctor, I took him at his word.

"I feel healthy," I said.

Dr. Yu proceeded to go over everything the previous doctor had covered, at which point I wasn't so much listening as meditating on the information.

"Statistically death occurs in less than one percent of patients," he was saying, and "If there is any indication of internal bleeding we might have to reopen."

I looked at him through doe-eyes caught in the brightly-lit headlights of glaring mortality.

"I see," I said.

"Do you have any questions?"

"Just one. Is there a reason we're doing this so late in the day? Aren't surgeries usually in the morning?"

"We need the organ to be transplanted as soon as possible for the highest likelihood of success. A kidney won't last very long, even on ice. Because your recipient is in..." he glanced down at his file, "New Jersey, they can prep him for an early morning surgery timed shortly after your kidney arrives on the East Coast."

"Ah, that makes sense."

"Is there anything else you'd like to know?"

"I think you both covered everything pretty thoroughly."

He extended his hand.

"Thank you, Eldonna, for what you are doing."

The receptionist led me back to the waiting room where Lana sat under a small Christmas tree decorated with silver ornaments, a thick folder resting in her lap. She patted the chair next to her.

"You feeling good about tomorrow, Eldonna?"

"I am."

She handed me a colorful chart with the names redacted.

"I thought you might like to have this. It shows the flow from you, the first person upstream, triggering the other surgeries down the line. As you know, your recipient is in New Jersey and his donor's kidney is going to Chicago. From there we think maybe another for a patient in San Diego. A complication has developed so we don't really know how far the chain will flow. Sometimes future transplants are delayed and end up happening long after the initial surgery, but the last kidney will go to someone on the UNOS waiting list."

"Thank you for this, Lana."

I pulled the bright green envelope from my purse and sealed it.

"I have a card for my recipient," I said. "Will you be sure he gets this by Christmas?" I realized my recipient could be Jewish or Muslim or something else but it still felt right since we were just days away from the holiday.

"Any communication has to go through the transplant center to protect everyone's privacy, but I'll send it along next week, okay?"

I ran my hand over the blank envelope.

"I can't even have a first name? I'd like to be thinking about him as I go into surgery and it would help to have a name."

"I'm sorry, no."

"Okay, well I've named him Frankie. *Frankie from New Joisey* sounds about right."

I handed her the envelope and she tucked it into her thick folder.

"Your surgery isn't until 4:00 so feel free to have a light meal early in the day tomorrow. I'll check in on you before you head into the operating room."

"Thank you for everything, Lana. You've made all of this a lot easier."

I rode the elevator down to the hospital lobby but decided to skip the shuttle and walk back to the hotel since the return trip was mostly downhill. I strolled past a public park dotted with napping San Franciscans and sniffing dogs on the ends of leashes. I turned left and slowly window-shopped a row of stores on my way toward the Kabuki. Not that I would buy anything even if I wanted something. Even if I could afford it. I might have mentioned I come from a family of penny-pinchers. My mother's people are predominantly Dutch, as was most of the population in the West Michigan area where I grew up. And they were the tightest of the tight. The joke went like this:

Q. How do you drive a Hollander crazy?

A. Put him in a round room and tell him there's a penny in the corner.

The unmistakable aroma of pizza wafted from a doorway and I followed it inside a small storefront echoing with banging pans and lively chatter. Although I rarely eat meat I ordered a slice of pepperoni, rationalizing it as a deserved reward for my long, hectic day. The pizza didn't make it a block in the box. I ate my way back to the hotel, grease running from the corners of my happy grin. The only thing that tastes better than a perfectly delicious slice is the knowledge that you got it for the special Thursday price of only $2.50, a dollar off regular price.

***

Mark showed up at the hotel at the exact minute he'd previously texted me with his ETA. Not a minute before or after. This ability to be so reliable, so precise, is the reason I chose him to be my "project manager" for the nephrectomy. As my medical advocate I knew he wouldn't let anyone get near me without first sanitizing their hands. As my Power of Attorney, he would be ready with pen in hand at any moment, to sign documents that might include pulling me off life support. And as my friend, he would offer the exact balance of support and mollycoddling I might require as my emotions shifted from one minute to the next leading up to and after surgery.

"Room service!" he announced from the other side of the hotel door.

"How was the drive?" I said, greeting him with a warm hug.

He set his bag on the bed closest to the door.

"We don't need to talk about that."

He was right; we didn't need to talk about it. I already knew he'd likely spent the last two hours cursing bad drivers as they sped past the man in the white SUV moving at exactly the speed limit, always signaling, not talking on his cell phone, and probably listening to Bach.

"So whatdja bring me?"

He unzipped the front packet of his suitcase and whipped out a book of Sunday crossword puzzles from the New York Times.

"Ta-da!"

It was one of our rituals and we fell into it easily—me propped up on pillows with reading glasses perched on my nose as he lovingly massaged my feet and answered the lion's share of clues.

"Five letters, Evita star, beginning with P."

"Peron," he said.

"Shit! I knew that one!"

"Sure you did. Give me your other leg."

He dipped into the massage cream and started on my right foot.

"So how are you feeling tonight? Are you nervous?"

"Not really. Maybe I should be but I'm not."

"Well it's either going to be fine or it isn't. The doctor could come out and say I've got good news and bad news. The good news is we harvested a kidney."

I beat him to the punch.

"And the bad news is we killed her but now we have a lot more organs to harvest!"

He was quiet for a minute and I knew that despite his pragmatism, he truly was concerned.

"You still sure you want to do this?"

"I have a good feeling about it," I said. "I think everything's going to be just fine."

I lay the crossword book across my chest and closed my eyes.

"I'm just going to enjoy this, okay?"

He playfully tugged on my blue-polished toe with a pink heart painted on the nail.

"Okay," he said.

We slept in the same bed. Neither of us was seeing anyone and it just felt right to fall asleep in the arms of the dearest, most loyal friend I knew, on the eve of what would be one of the riskiest and most important days of my life.

NINETEEN

December 16, 2010

When I woke the next morning Mark was already on coffee duty, brewing a pot in the room with the provided carafe. I sat up in bed and accepted his goodwill with low expectations for greatness but a high expectation for the needed pick-me-up. The coffee was just so-so but the caffeine got me moving as far as the bathroom where I pulled on a pair of leggings and a sweater, then stepped into pink Uggs before we headed downstairs together.

The café attached to the hotel lobby stood nearly empty, save for three waitresses rushing around as if it were full. We slid into a booth where I ordered an espresso while my companion loaded up on eggs, pancakes, and other various pastries and meats at the breakfast bar.

I glanced down at his plate.

"Bacon *and* sausage?"

Mark wiped his mouth with a napkin and took a sip of his coffee.

"Yeah unfortunately they were all out of *tofu*. You should eat something," he said, pointing at my empty plate with his fork. "You'll need your energy today."

"I'm not hungry."

"You will be."

"Nothing looks good to me."

"It's complimentary," he said, appealing to my frugality.

I took a bite of his toast and put it back on his plate.

"Nope."

"Pastry?"

"Too sweet."

"Hash browns?"

"Too greasy."

"Ok, don't say I didn't try."

I watched as he cleaned his plate, tucking an apple into his jacket pocket before zipping it up.

"Shall we go for a walk?"

"Sure. I'd like to look for a store where I can pick up some Tums or something. My stomach feels queasy."

"Nerves?"

"Maybe. Or maybe that pizza yesterday."

He held my jacket while I slipped my arm into the sleeves, double-wrapping a scarf around my neck. I stuck my hands into fingerless gloves and clapped them together.

"You ready, Nanook?"

"Hey, it's cold in this city."

He shook his head.

"You're such a delicate flower. I don't know how you survived all those years in Michigan."

"I survived but I wouldn't say I thrived. I've always believed the stork dropped me on the wrong body of water."

We walked out of the restaurant and down a long hallway that took us into Japantown, an indoor mall of sorts, lined with Asian import shops and sushi bars. I stopped in front of a glass-front spa. Inside, white-uniformed girls with black ponytails leaned over businessmen and women, plying muscles with their pointy elbows.

"Would you like a shiatsu massage?"

"Nah, I prefer hand on skin instead of bone through layers of clothing."

One of the girls looked at me through the window and I smiled at her. She stared past me, her penetrating eyes and firmly set mouth never changing. Maybe it was one-way glass and she didn't really see me but I don't think so. I imagine it was similar to how caged animals must feel. I wondered if she resented the bright lights and the constant intrusion of curious strangers on her life.

"It's their culture," Mark said, as if reading my mind. "A smile from a stranger has a different meaning than it does for an American."

"I don't think I'd thrive in Japan any better than in the frozen north. Both seem really cold."

"It's actually a beautiful country. You just have to respect the differences. Not everyone is as happy-go-lucky as you are."

I slapped him on the arm.

"And not everyone is as serious as you are."

"Come on my hothouse flower. Let's get you something for that upset stomach."

We made our way out of the enclosed mall past a theater and over a bridge to Safeway, me with my chin bent to my chest against the cold wind.

"You should have worn your hat," Mark said, wrapping my scarf over my mouth as we left the store with our purchases. He opened the package and handed me two fruit-flavored tablets. I chewed them quickly before sticking my hand back out. He shook out a couple more tablets into my glove and smirked.

"I told you you'd get hungry."

Back at the hotel we boarded the shuttle, arriving at the hospital a couple hours before surgery, per the instructions on my itinerary. While waiting in front of the elevator I caught the reflection of a fifty one year-old woman with magenta pigtails poking out from under a grey knit hat, pink yarn-balls hanging from its strings, no make-up, wearing a sweatshirt and slippers under yoga pants. Except for the hat I looked like I was heading for a slumber party. In a way I suppose I was. At the very least I was about to have a nice long nap.

We got out at the sixth floor where Lana waiting for us.

"Good morning, Eldonna. How are you feeling?"

"I'm good. How are you?"

"Excited." She said. "I'd like you to meet your admitting nurse."

I shook the woman's hand, reading her tag.

"Hi, KaRonda. It's good to meet you."

"It's good to meet you, too. Are you ready to get started?"

"As ready as I'll ever be."

Lana touched my shoulder.

"I'll come find you before surgery, okay?"

"Okay. See you in a while."

Mark and I followed KaRonda down a long hallway to a tiny admitting room outfitted with a bed, a row of cabinets, and a single padded chair.

"Take everything off including any jewelry and put your things in here," she said, handing me a plastic bag. "Then put this gown on and get into the bed."

I did as I was told except that instead of the provided hospital slippers, I pulled on the wooly purple Tibetan socks that Dominique had sent from India. Not only were they snuggly on my feet, I felt the warmth of her friendship walking with me as I was about to take the last few steps on this nearly four-year journey.

KaRonda returned for my things and noted the little statuette of K'Wan Yin on the table.

"How about I put that on your bedside stand when you're out of surgery?"

"Promise?"

"I promise."

She added the statue to my bag along with my clothes and the mala beads that hadn't left my wrist since Dominique sent them. KaRonda disappeared and another admitting nurse replaced my beads with a hospital wristband.

My phone beeped with a message notification and I

flipped it open with my right hand. Despite our not finding a matched pair, Kathy and Jim were sending blessings for a successful outcome. I held the phone to my chest and sighed.

The nurse clipped a monitor over my left forefinger.

"Everything okay?"

"Yes," I said. "Just a friend wishing me well."

"Your vitals look good but your blood pressure is pretty low for someone about to have major surgery. Did you have a good last meal?"

Mark laughed.

"You might want to rephrase that," he said.

The nurse clapped her hand over her mouth.

"Oh dear! That came out wrong!"

"I wasn't very hungry," I said, laughing.

A whoosh of hot air blew across my skin as she pushed a button above a hose attached to my hospital gown.

"Whoa!"

"We pump warm air in there to keep you from getting chilly."

"Well you might want to turn it down before I start hot-flashing and rip my gown off."

She laughed and flipped the switch.

"Sorry. Usually people get cold in here."

"I'm good. I'll let you know if I cool down too much."

"Okay." She handed me a clipboard. "I just need you to sign here verifying your permission for us to remove your left kidney. Do you have a health care directive and someone with power of attorney?"

"Right here," Mark said, raising his hand like an obedient student.

"It's all in my file," I added.

"Church or minister?"

"None."

"Person to call?"

I pointed to Mark who raised his hand again.

"I'll be here as long as I'm needed."

"Okay, then I think we're all set. I'm just going to get your I.V. ready to keep you in fluids and medication during surgery." She slipped a needle into the back of my hand and attached it to a closed tubular capsule. "You can just take it easy until we're ready for you."

"I'll be right here," I said.

When she left the room I flipped open my phone and dialed up my son. I waited for him to turn down music in the background before speaking.

"Hello?"

"Hey, it's me. I just wanted you to know that you don't need to drive up from Santa Cruz tonight."

The signal died and the phone went dead. I looked over at Mark.

"Shoot. I lost him but I don't want to call back because it sounds like he's driving."

Before Mark could answer the phone rang.

"Sorry. A cop was driving by. It's not a problem to drive up there tonight after class."

"I'll probably be asleep until morning, Honey. You can come see me tomorrow, okay? Mark will call you when I'm out of surgery."

"Okay, well tell Mark to call me if anything…"

"Everything will be fine. I just wanted to tell you I love you and not to worry."

"I love you too, Mom."

I waited for him to hang up first like I always do. As soon as I heard the click the flood came.

Mark sprang from his chair.

"What's wrong?"

"I don't know. I love him so much and I just realized how hard this must be for him, worrying that he could lose his mother for no other reason than she decided to give away a kidney. I know I'll be fine but I also know how close to the chest he holds his cards. I'm guessing he's probably a bit of a wreck right now and I hate that I'm causing him to suffer."

"You want to call him back?"

"No. He'll be more concerned if he hears me crying."

He handed me a tissue.

"Can I get you anything? Some water?"

I didn't answer.

"Chocolate? Dancing clowns?"

I smiled through my tears.

"I think I just need a minute."

Lana walked in, took one look at me, then politely asked Mark and the nurse, who'd stopped by to check my vitals again, to leave the room before closing the door. She approached the bed and put her hand on my shoulder.

"Are you okay?"

I wiped my eyes with the edge of the hospital gown and nodded.

"It's not too late to change your mind, you know. We can tell the recipient there was a problem with the final blood match. They don't have to know you decided not to donate."

I shook my head.

"I'm not crying because I'm scared. I'm just feeling...emotional."

Lana leaned over the rail, her hand moving to grasp mine.

"Eldonna—"

"Okay, maybe I'm a little scared but that's not the reason for the tears. I think it just hit me how big a thing this is, the reality of it all finally happening after nearly four years of waiting."

"It is a big thing Eldonna. A very big thing. And frankly I'd be more concerned if you *weren't* having this moment. It tells me you're in touch with what's going on, that you're a participant rather than a bystander. As your transplant coordinator I find that reassuring."

I looked from her eyes to her expanding belly and smiled.

"You're really starting to show. I've been so wrapped up

in all the last-minute tests and prep I forgot to congratulate you on your upcoming miracle."

"Well I suppose I could say the same thing to you now, couldn't I? You're about to give someone a new life and that's pretty miraculous."

"Yeah, I guess it is."

"Eldonna, I need to ask you one more time. Do you still want to go through with it?"

I thought about Kathy. I thought about Alice. I thought about the man in New Jersey whom I'd never met and the seventeen people who would die today because they hadn't received a needed organ in time.

I squeezed Lana's hand.

"I do. I'm ready. Let's go."

She tucked a stray pink hair under my hospital cap and nodded.

"Okay. Let's go."

I thought they'd roll me on a cart to the operating arena but I walked down the hall in my socks, stopping first at a small room for a last-minute interview with the anesthesiologist. The young, Hollywood-handsome dude was cute but ruined the cuteness a little by being so aware of it. I imagine it might be difficult to emerge from one's twenties with an impressive medical degree, a job at a respected big city hospital, plus drop-dead gorgeous looks, without having one's ego move to the front of the room.

"Hello, Eldonna. I'm Doctor Whittaker*." He sat on a stool and scooted closer so we were face-to-face. "I'm going to be your drug dealer for the little trip you're about to take."

Ha. So he was funny, too. It was really hard not to like him despite the silver spoon sticking out of his perfect mouth.

"Hi," was all I could manage.

"I went over your file and it looks like you don't have any allergies so I'm just going to explain what you can expect once we're inside, okay?"

"Okay."

"First, I'll give you something to relax. Then a little oxygen before I inject the cocktail we use to keep you sedated during the procedure. From then on I'll monitor your vitals very closely and adjust as needed." He checked his watch. "Is there anything you'd like to ask me?"

"Does anyone ever wake up in the middle of surgery?"

I had no idea where that question came from other than perhaps having read it somewhere. Funny how your hidden fears pop up spontaneously like that.

He pointed with two fingers toward his eyes, then mine, then back to his.

"I've got you, Eldonna. It's just you and me in there in terms of your sedation. You won't wake up until the recovery room when we slowly bring you back. I promise you that."

"Okay."

He put a hand on my shoulder and repeated the two-finger thing back and forth between our eyes.

"Just you and me," he repeated.

I nodded and he squeezed my upper arm.

"One more thing," he said. "I like to listen to music in the operating room. It helps the time go by. Now's your chance to choose the score for the opening act of your surgery."

"Oh, cool. How about *In the Arms of the Angels* by Sarah McLachlan?"

"Hmm," he said, turning to look through his digital library. "I think I have that."

"Wait," I said. "That song is fucking depressing. Play *Here Comes The Sun*."

He whirled around in his chair and flashed that movie-star grin. "Now you're talkin'!"

Mark was waiting in the hallway next to a surgical nurse, who stood by while we said our goodbyes.

"I've got your back," he said as we embraced. "I'll be

waiting for you as soon as you're awake."

"Thank you for everything. I love you."

The nurse looped her arm around my waist and led me toward a pair of big double doors. Of all the things to enter my mind at that moment, I suddenly realized that I was supposed to usher a concert with *The Blind Boys of Alabama* at the PAC that night and couldn't recall if I'd let anyone know I wouldn't be there.

The last thing I remember is climbing onto the operating table in a brightly-lit room furnished in glass and polished stainless, big round lights on cables hanging over sterile blue sheets. I smelled oxygen, saw a sea of smiling faces, felt various hands touching, adjusting, reassuring, heard The Beatles singing, *it's all right; sun, sun, sun, here it comes…*

***

I'm not what you'd call a religious person. From the moment I left the comfort of my father's religion I began a haphazard journey toward a higher truth than what I perceived as his flawed dogma. Beginning in my late twenties and winding down in my mid-forties, I latched onto a spiritual pendulum that swung from Native American Studies to Metaphysics to Buddhism, gulping down words and rituals I hoped would slake my existential thirst, only to end up more parched than ever.

Not that I didn't find some truth in each of my quests for spiritual enlightenment. I did. But mostly I found a plethora of people whose walk didn't match their talk. Most of the so-called gurus I met practiced hypocrisy through the mere existence of their self-proclaimed titles. To my mind an "old soul" would never tell you they were an old soul any more than a Magi would need to advertise his sagacity. In doing so the ego steps forward in complete contradiction to the larger truth. Anyone can regurgitate talking points. What's difficult, and feels truly enlightened, is the act of living those words.

The other resulting epiphany from my spiritual quest was that most of the teachings I unearthed were simply different ways of modeling Christ's teachings of love, compassion, and tolerance, as well as others who came before him with the same message. Unlike the self-described instruments of religion who exercise habits of righteous indignation and condemnation, Christ's lessons were about acceptance. From lepers to prostitutes, he not only preached compassion, he embraced others rather than abandoning them for their shortcomings or imperfections.

What I couldn't know when I rebelled against my religious upbringing is that my search for truth would bring me full circle, back to words from a book I continue to reject *literally* but now embrace in essence, most specifically, the Golden Rule. Or in the verse I like better from I John 3:18, *"Let us love, not in word or speech, but in truth and action."* To that end I have tried, and failed, and continue trying to live a life of love with a capital L.

As my fellow ushers back in SLO were letting out the last patrons and locking up the PAC doors, surgeons would be ushering my left kidney out of my body and toward its intended recipient. I don't need to affiliate with a particular religion to appreciate the fact that although I wasn't aware of it at the time, from California to Colorado to Michigan to Maine, hundreds of people were praying for me that day. My daughter met with my niece to pray. My sisters prayed. Their church members prayed. Even my online writing community enveloped me in a circle of protection that they'd created to virtually hold me in the light as I was about to drift off under anesthesia.

Joan Osborne once posed the question, "What if God was one of us?" To her, and to you, I would ask, "What if God was *all* of us?"

***

The first thing I remember upon waking from surgery was feeling like I couldn't get air.

"I can't breathe," I whispered.

A nurse bent close to my face.

"You're breathing, Eldonna. You're okay."

"I. Can't. Breathe." I repeated it one word at a time and each syllable took one hundred percent of my effort. My throat felt like it was closing.

"What's wrong?" It was Mark's voice. When I opened my eyes I'm certain he saw the panic. "She can't breathe," he said, holding my hand.

"Sir, we need you to step outside."

He kissed my cheek.

"I'll see you in a little bit."

"Please don't go."

I felt his hand leave mine before everything went black again.

TWENTY

December 17, 2010

The next time I woke was in a regular hospital room. My throat felt like sun-dried beach sand at low tide and I could barely swallow. I reached around in hopes of finding water somewhere nearby and was instantly reminded by a sharp pain in my abdomen that I probably didn't want to make any moves right then, sudden or otherwise.

Mark leapt from his chair at the end of the bed.

"What do you need?"

"Water," I croaked.

He placed a bent straw to my lips and I pulled on it but most of the water dribbled back down my chin and onto my gown.

"I can't swallow."

"I'll see if I can get you some ice chips."

He returned within a couple minutes carrying a small styrofoam cup.

"Try this," he said, folding my hands around it.

The ice felt like snow angels kissing my throat.

"Where am I?"

"You're in a regular hospital room. They moved you here from the recovery room sometime during the night."

"You should go get some sleep," I whispered, not knowing how late he'd stayed with me after the surgery.

"I shall. As soon as I'm confident that you're alright.

You had me pretty worried there for a while last night."

"Why? Did it go okay?"

"The surgery? Yes. But you had a heck of a time coming out of the anesthesia."

"I don't remember much."

A nurse arrived to check my vitals.

"Are you in pain?" she asked.

I nodded.

"We have you hooked up to a self-administering morphine pump." She pressed a small button into my hand. "Just push this with your thumb when the pain gets too uncomfortable. Don't worry about overmedicating, you can't get a dose more than once every ten minutes and it's programmed to stop at the maximum dose for your height and weight."

I didn't care about the pain so much as my dry throat at that moment.

"Ice, please," I said.

The nurse handed me back the cup and I scraped a few chips into my mouth with my teeth before she took it away again.

"You need to rest now." She looked over at Mark who moved to the head of the bed and kissed me on the forehead.

"I'm going back to the hotel to take a nap. I'll be back to check on you later."

I nodded, too tired to speak.

"The nurse's station has my number. Have them call me if you run into any problems or need me to come back, okay?"

My eyelids drooped over my eyeballs. I might have hit the morphine button a couple of times. I wanted to thank him but my mouth was too dry to form words. I wanted to grab his hand but every time I moved a deep pain shot from under my left rib to my pelvis.

"G'bye," was all I managed before drifting back to sleep.

***

I woke a couple hours later with my throat still irritated and a killer headache to go along with it. When people ask about the recovery, what I remember most is the dry throat and the headache more than any pain at the surgical site. My abdomen hurt when I moved or tried to prop myself up but it was my head and throat that had my immediate attention. No matter how many times I hit the opiate button the throbbing in my brain pan persisted.

"Could I have a little coffee?" I asked a nurse as she checked my bandages.

"No, sorry. Just water and jello today."

Mark returned as she was checking the bag at the end of the bed.

"Really good urine output, Eldonna," she said. "Your remaining kidney is working well."

I pictured my right kidney waking up, yawning, noticing the extra fluids from surgery then turning to greet her sister only to find a few staples and going, *What the hell? You ditched and left me with all this work to do by myself?*

Mark waved at me from the foot of the bed then glanced toward the nurse. "How's she doing?"

"We took blood during the night—you mostly slept through it, Eldonna—and your creatinine and GFR are normal for post-nephrectomy."

"Yay, me," I half-whispered. "How's the other guy?"

"All I know is that the surgery was successful and he's putting out urine which means your kidney kicked right in. He's a lucky guy."

"*His* kidney, not mine. No longer belongs to me."

When she left, Mark moved toward the head of the bed.

"Tell the truth. How are you really feeling?"

"My throat is still super dry. It's all I can do just to swallow crushed ice. But this headache. Ugh. Will you sneak me some coffee?"

He frowned.

"You know I can't do that if they said you can't have it."

I felt like a drug addict bargaining with her dealer.

"They said I could have clear fluids."

"Can't they give you something for the headache? It is a hospital after all."

The woman in the next bed started hacking. It turned into a five-minute coughing fit, each one sending an arrow through my skull.

"I'm already higher than a kite on morphine or whatever they've got in that bag but my head still hurts like hell."

He brushed my bangs off my forehead.

"It'll be gone soon, I bet. Probably just stress."

"Maybe." We waited through another coughing seizure from my sick neighbor. "Thanks for coming up. You get a nap?"

"I did. How about you?"

"Slept like a drunk on payday. I kept thinking I'd have to pee but there's a cath."

"I know. I saw it."

"Oh. Sorry."

"No big deal."

I thumbed the button for the third time in thirty minutes, sending a whoosh of sleepiness over me.

"I'm a little tired."

"Of course you are. Go to sleep. I have to head back to Monterey to work for a bit but I'll be back tomorrow. I spoke with Jacob and he'll be here later this afternoon."

I drifted in and out of sleep, mostly out, until a nurse came by with a tray of food. I managed a few sips of broth and a couple bites of the jello before giving up. My throat was too sore and I had no appetite. When she returned half an hour later and saw how little I'd eaten she frowned.

"That's it?"

I wrinkled my nose and nodded.

"Okay, then let's get you on your feet. The sooner

you're up and walking the faster you'll heal."

She cranked my bed and I groaned.

"Ow."

"Come on, now. You can do this." She lifted my legs and turned my body so my feet dangled above the floor, with one hand behind my back to support me.

"Ow, ow, ow," was all I could manage. I felt every movement in every stitch and staple and in other places I'd forgotten existed.

"Put your arm around my shoulder. We'll go up really slowly."

I did as I was told, keeping my right hand across my abdomen to support it.

"We're gonna stand on three," she said.

I braced myself as she counted.

"One. Two. Three!" she said, straining to pull me up. She succeeded in getting me to my feet by propping me there but all my weight was on her shoulder and the arm beneath mine.

"I think I'm going to pass out," I said, and I meant it. Having lived my whole life with low blood pressure I know when my legs are about to give. I started to buckle and she sat me back on the bed.

"I might throw up," I squeaked.

"You're okay." She helped me back into a reclining position. "We'll try again later," she said, before moving to check on the coughing patient in the next bed.

I'm not okay, I thought. But I didn't say it out loud. Growing up, the rule in our house went something like this: Unless you puke, pass out, have a visible rash, or your fever is above one hundred degrees, you're still going to school/church/whatever you're trying to get out of doing. For some unknown reason it was automatically assumed we were faking if we complained of not feeling well. We even had a name for it: Falsey Judas (pronounced *folzee judiss*) I'm sure there was some biblical correlation but it was lost on me. Still is. But what did follow me into my adult life was that somehow acknowledging sickness is a weakness. And despite knowing better on an intellectual level I'm guilty of having accused my own children of faking illnesses. Not that they never did it but I felt like a heel those times the school called to ask why I sent my sick kid to classes.

In all fairness, I've held myself up to the same standard, refusing to take to my bed or visit a doctor unless I think I'm dying. It's not a martyr thing. In fact, I hide how bad I'm feeling. Take for instance some unknown irritant that randomly decided to waft its way into my universe after never having manifested so much as a single allergic reaction to anything ever. A couple years after moving to California I started scratching my eyeballs out trying to assuage the constant prickling. I woke with my nose stuffed fuller than a grocery bag on dollar day at the Goodwill. My blotchy wet face looked like I'd just watched *Brian's Song*, *Beaches*, and *Philadelphia* back to back with an *Old Yeller* chaser. And still I remained in denial until I was finally diagnosed with a pollen allergy.

"I'm sorry," I said to the nurse when she returned to cover me with a blanket. "I tried. I really did."

"It's okay, Honey. We'll give it another go tomorrow."

But as she reclined the bed I swear I heard a chorus of voices behind me whispering, *Folzee Judisssss!*

***

When I woke again later that evening the fierce headache remained. It was all I could do to focus on my son, who stood at my bedside.

"Hey Mom. How are you doing?"

"Pretty good. They say everything went really well."

"You look like hell," he said, and laughed. "Just kidding. You look good for someone who just had part of her guts removed."

"Ow! Don't make me laugh," I said, holding my belly.

"Sorry."

"It's okay. I'm really glad you came. Was the traffic bad?"

"Horrible, but I'm a good driver. I keep telling you that."

"I know you are," I fibbed. I didn't know it but I did want to believe him.

He moved nearer to my face.

"You want me to have them turn that lady's TV down?" he whispered.

I shook my head.

"I don't want to cause any trouble."

"Mom, you need your rest," he said quietly. "Between her yelling on the phone and hacking..."

I smiled at my son, who'd seemingly evolved into a responsible young man in the short time he'd gone off to UCSC.

"It's okay. Really."

"You look tired."

"I am. I don't think I can stay awake much longer but I'm so glad you came up." As much as I loved having my son visit, I was feeling more drained with every word.

"I'm staying overnight at the Kabuki. Mark gave me his room for the night so I could come see you again in the morning before I have to go home."

"I love you," I whispered.

He kissed me.

"I love you too, Mom. I'll be back in the morning, okay?"

I nodded, tears welling up in my eyes.

"You want me to stay?"

"No, it's the drugs. They make me weepy."

He grinned.

"I bet they're giving you some good shit, huh? Enjoy the buzz," he said, and kissed me again, then gave my curtained neighbor a glaring stink-eye before quietly stepping out the door.

Mark called before bedtime to check in with me.

"How are you feeling? Was Jacob able to find you?"

"A little better tonight. Jacob was here but I was really tired so we didn't visit long."

"Did they get you out of bed today?"

"They tried. I failed."

"How's your head?"

"Still hurts like hell."

"And the incision?"

"Really sore but only when I move or when I laugh."

"Well fortunately for you I'm more of a funny *hmmm* guy than a funny ha-ha guy."

"Ouch," I laughed. "You're mostly funny when you don't mean to be."

"You get some sleep. I'll see you tomorrow, okay?"

"Okay. Thanks for checking on me."

"Of course."

I closed my phone and set it on the bed table. My roommate had tuned into some sort of cop drama and every bullet felt like it went straight through my forehead. I hit another dose of the magic morphine button and sailed off to sleep.

TWENTY-ONE

December 18, 2010

An orderly and a nurse stood on either side of my bed and rolled me down the hall to a small room at the very end of the hospital floor. My head still jangled with pain but the relief of being moved to where it was quiet, no hacking, and no TV, was a welcome balm.

"Thank you so much," I said.

The nurse checked my morphine pump and locked the wheels on my bed.

"Don't thank us," she said, "Thank the public relations director. He stopped by to see you yesterday and was really pissed to find our first non-directed donor in a shared room."

"I don't remember seeing him."

"You were pretty out of it."

When she finished making notes on her clipboard I asked her to hand me my laptop before she left. I'd mentioned on Facebook that I'd be out of commission for a while due to a brief hospital stay. Other than my family and closest friends I hadn't initially told many what I was doing. Several people had messaged me privately to say they hoped it wasn't anything serious. Rather than reply to each one of them I'd finally spilled the beans the day before surgery. *I'm not sick*, I wrote, *I'm donating a kidney. Thanks for all your good wishes and concerns. I'll check in next week.*

A lump formed in my throat when I opened Facebook to

discover that all six of my siblings had changed their profile pictures to photos of me at different ages in my life. I scrolled through pages and pages of posts wishing me well. And when I jumped over to the online journaling community with whom I'd been writing and sharing for over a decade, the lump turned into a flood: *Let's all gather around her bed and beam our love at her. She'll know we're there.* From there the thread expanded by a couple dozen replies, all sending good wishes my way.

I've always considered myself a fairly independent person, to the point of being stubbornly stoic rather than ask for help. As a result I sometimes assume I'm mostly alone during those times when I'm in pain or afraid. My heart nearly folded over on itself as I read emails from friends as far as the UK, Facebook posts from family members who live over two thousand miles away, and acquaintances I hardly knew. I can't remember when I've felt so loved, so completely surrounded with tenderness and genuine concern.

Jacob walked in to find me sitting in front of my laptop, bawling.

"Is something wrong or are the drugs still making you weepy?"

"Nothing's wrong," I said. "I'm just a sentimental idiot."

He sat next to the bed.

"You may be sentimental but you're no idiot."

I closed my computer and he set it aside. His curls were still damp from a shower and it was all I could do not to reach out and comb my fingers through them, something he's always hated but tolerated nonetheless.

"Nice digs," he said, glancing around the room.

"Right? I thought you'd complained but it turned out to be someone from PR."

"It's the least they can do considering what you did."

"The least they could do is let me have coffee."

"Head still hurting?"

I nodded.

A nurse interrupted us to check my vitals.

"You move your bowels yet, Ms. Edwards?"

Jacob instantly stood.

"Hey I need to make a quick call to work. I'll be right back," he said as he slowly backed out of the room.

I glanced out the hospital window and back to the nurse. Just the thought of straining after surgery, even a little bit, made me woozy. I shook my head.

"Um, that would be a no."

"We can't let you go home until it happens. Would you like a stool softener?"

"Sure. Not making any promises, though."

She put the blood pressure cuff back in its sleeve and made a note on her clipboard.

"I realize the idea sounds a little scary when you're abdomen is so tender but the fear is worse than the actual event."

I adjusted myself on the pillows propped behind me.

"If you say so," I said, unconvinced.

"I'll be back in a while to take you for a walk. Moving around will help all your systems heal faster."

She made it sound like we were going for a stroll on the boardwalk, as if putting one foot in front of the other supporting all my weight on said foot was no big deal.

"Oh goody," I said.

Jacob returned as the nurse was leaving.

"Mark just called to say he's on his way. He should be here in a couple hours."

My son looked around the room, his eyes landing on the bronze-colored statue that sat on the bedside table next to a bouquet of roses from Lana.

"What's that?"

"K'wan Yin, the bodhisattva of compassion."

"I see," he said, his standard answer for anything he didn't care to know more about.

"You have to work today?"

"Actually, I do. I wish I could stay longer but I want to get one more day in before I drive back to SLO to help take care of you."

"No worries, Honey. I'm so glad to see you when I can actually form a sentence."

"Yeah, you were a zombie yesterday."

"I don't remember much. But despite feeling drugged I knew you were here and that means a lot to me."

He moved to kiss me on the cheek.

"I'll call you later, alright?"

"Okay. Drive as if they're trying to kill you."

"Pretty sure they are. San Francisco drivers are the worst."

The nurse returned as he was leaving.

"You must be proud of your mom," she said.

He glanced toward me then back at her.

"Yup," he said.

My son is a man of few words.

"Don't worry, we'll take good care of her," she said.

I watched for as long as I could see the back of his corduroy blazer, until he turned a corner toward the bank of elevators.

"Nice boy. It's obvious how much he loves you."

"He's a good kid. He's got a good heart."

"Must take after his mom," she said. "I don't know about your heart but from what I hear your kidney is working like a champ in the new guy."

"His kidney," I reminded her. For some reason it bugged me to think of it as mine once I'd given it away. I didn't want to claim ownership of it anymore. Maybe I worried that I'd feel guilty if it failed at some point or if there were other complications. I wished I could have slapped a tag on the side of it that read, *As-Is, no refunds*!

My nurse encouraged me to eat a little jello and some clear broth.

"We need to get you out of bed before the end of the

day. So you'll need some energy."

I looked at her like she'd just asked me to run a marathon. I could barely sit up without pain stopping me in mid-movement. Plus I still had the raging headache.

"I'll try. But I'm pretty sure I can't walk."

"Not as well with this catheter in. Doc says it's okay to remove it now. Take a deep breath and on the count of three blow out."

She started counting before I had a chance to think about it. I sucked in a breath and blew.

"That didn't hurt at all," I said.

"Eat up," she said, and wheeled the hospital table back in front of me.

A male nurse about my age returned an hour later. He noted the nearly-finished broth and jello.

"Got your appetite back, I see."

"A little. Hey, I have to pee," I said. "Can you bring me something to use?"

"The bathroom is only a few steps away. I'd like to see you try that."

My brain was resistant but my bladder was like a cheerleader, *let's go, let's go, l-e-t-s-g-o!*

"Okay. Let's give it a whirl."

I did my best not to groan too much as he helped me turn, then steadied me to my feet.

"Woo-hoo!" I said, weaving. "I'm a little high."

"I've got you." He grabbed my arm. "Slowly now, one step at a time."

We inched our way to the bathroom where he set a container over the stool to catch my urine so it could be measured and tested.

"Hold onto the bar. I'll be right outside the door if you need me."

It never felt so good to pee. And pee and pee and pee. It hurt to stand but with the help of the bar I managed, pulling my IV along with me as I took my first unassisted step.

"Okay, I'm done."

By the time he got me back into bed I was exhausted but pleased.

"Good job," he said. "Try to ease up on the drugs if you can manage so you'll be a little steadier on your feet when we get you walking a bit further today."

Dr. Bry arrived, chart in hand.

"How are you feeling, Ms. Edwards?"

"Pretty good. I've had a headache ever since yesterday morning but the abdominal pain is manageable with the morphine."

"The headache could be a side effect from the anesthesia. Give it a couple of days and it will probably dissipate. Your GFR continues to improve, which shows that your right kidney has stepped up to take up the slack. The creatinine is a little high but well within range for post-surgery." He set the chart down on the table and pulled back the sheet to expose the incision sites. "No indication of infection. I know it feels a little like you've been kicked in the stomach but a week from now you'll be down to a couple Tylenol." He covered me back up.

"When can I go back to work?"

"We like to you to wait six to eight weeks. I'll have a better idea when we see you at your two-week checkup. Keep in mind the body heals quickly but it can take up to six months for the effects of anesthesia to completely leave your system. You might feel more tired than usual for a while so you'll want to take it easy." He glanced at his watch. "Barring any complications you can probably go home on Monday."

"Thank you. And thank you for your expertise."

"You're welcome. It was teamwork—lots of doctors and nurses working together for this outcome. We're just happy you were willing to donate and glad you're doing so well."

An hour after Dr. Bry left, my nurse returned.

"Ready to try a little walk?"

"Not really but I'll give it a go."

I did better than I expected but not as well as the nurse would have liked. The faster I tried to move, the more it felt like trying to rush honey off a spoon. I barely managed a Tim Conway shuffle about halfway to the nurse's station before needing to sit down. I rested for five minutes in a chair, then slippered my way back to the room where I immediately fell back to sleep, exhausted.

I didn't wake until Mark arrived in the early evening.

"Hi there," he said. "How's our patient?"

"Tired," I said.

"Did you expect to be doing yoga and dancing today?"

"No, but I have to admit I was a little unprepared for the level of fatigue."

"You just had major surgery Ellie."

"I know. I just see myself as so invincible. Pretty silly, huh?"

He retrieved a bottle of lotion from the drawer in my bedside table and lifted the end of the blanket to expose my left foot.

"You like to put on a tough front but you're not fooling me."

He pulled off my sock then squirted lotion into his hands before rubbing them together to warm it. My eyes rolled backward at the sheer pleasure of his firm grip on my heel as he folded his knuckles into the sole of my foot.

You'd think a massage therapist would never take for granted the power of human touch but sometimes I do. Sometimes I get so caught up in the day-to-day demands of heading a household and massaging all those needy bodies that I lose my own place at the table. Massage therapists often claim they're not healers but merely vessels for healing. The downside to this belief is that in order to let that big of a love flow through one's body she must, to a degree, get out of her own way. When you get it right, when every moment feels like a dance between you, the gods, and one of their precious children, it's better than any dopamine-induced trip you'll ever take.

Like most highs, in order to reach nirvana you sometimes take leave of your own body. And occasionally you forget to come back. For me, all it takes is a tender reach, a simple hand on my back or a squeezed shoulder to send me keening toward home, that place within my body where the marriage of cell and soul feels complete. Somewhere inside these moments I remember why I do what I do and why, if I'm starved for touch, I simply cannot give to others from an empty well.

As Mark lovingly rubbed my feet I turned my head and came face to face with my little bronze bodhisattva. Her hands rest in her lap, eyes closed in quiet meditation. She looks peaceful and yet there's this tiny smile, a bit sweet and a bit impish, that punctuates her face. It's almost as if she's just heard a joke or is hiding a secret. As I studied her I recalled the parable of the bodhisattva finding water in the desert. The more I reflected on the story the more I realized that we are all of us little buddhas in our own way. I thought about my recipient and how our doctors, our friends, our families—mine and his—had arrived at this oasis together. Or as Ram Das once said, "We are all just walking each other home."

TWENTY-TWO

December 19, 2010

I woke to Mark sitting in a chair in the corner of the hospital room reading the San Francisco Chronicle.

"Well, good morning, princess" He neatly folded his newspaper. "How are you feeling?"

"My head hurts."

'Still?"

"Would you *please*?"

He started to object then sighed.

"Alright. But if they bust me I'm gonna sing."

He returned within forty-five minutes with a double tall mocha latte. I drank it down and handed him the empty cup.

"Oh. My. God. Thank you so much."

He wiped the foam off my upper lip and shook his head.

"You're such an addict."

"Even Starbucks tastes good at this point."

"And you're such a snob."

"There are only three things in this world I'm picky about: a perfectly pulled macchiato with just the right amount of crema, a deep tissue massage from a skilled therapist, and 600 thread-count Egyptian cotton sheets. I could live in a shack and be happy if I only had extraordinary coffee, awesome massage, and decadent sheets."

"Well you're going to have to settle for hospital sheets, corporate coffee and *my* hands for the time being."

"You give great foot!"

He smiled.

"That means a lot, coming from you."

An orderly arrived with breakfast but the coffee had filled me up. I ate half a bagel and drank the juice then pushed the tray toward Mark.

"Can you finish this?"

He bent over the plate and heartily cleaned the rest of my breakfast. His thick wavy hair had turned from silver to nearly white in the time I'd known him but his Groucho Marx eyebrows remained dark and animated, dancing above his eyes as he chewed.

"I guess you were hungry."

"I'm a project manager," he said, grinning. "I hate waste."

I glanced at the empty Starbucks cup and grinned.

"Please sir, could I have another?"

He stood, shaking his head.

"You need rehab," he said, and headed out the door.

A nurse arrived to change out my I.V. bag.

"How's the headache?"

It occurred to me that for the first time since I'd awakened from surgery my head wasn't pounding.

"It's good!" I nearly yelled. "I feel great!"

She glanced at the empty coffee cup on the night stand and perched her hands on her hips, pretending to be mad.

"Well in that case are you ready to try another walk?"

"I am, actually."

She helped me to the bathroom then followed me for a few steps as I inched my way down the hall, holding the I.V. stand like a staff to steady me. I won't lie, it hurt. But not as bad as the first time and I could actually feel my body thanking me for the movement. I rested at the far end of the hall then turned to make my way back. When Mark stepped off the elevator he nearly jumped in surprise.

"Well, look at you. Guess you won't be needing *this*."

He put the coffee cup to his lips and pretended to drink.

"Give me that!" I said, swiping at the air as he held the coffee out of my reach.

"Come and get it," he said, walking backwards, carrot in hand, grinning.

It worked. I made it to the room without stopping. As soon as I was back in bed, Mark rewarded me with my second latte' and I drank it down nearly as quickly as the first. I handed him the empty cup and ran my fingers through my stringy hair.

"I feel so gross," I said. "I haven't had a bath since Thursday."

A nurse returned to check my vitals, post-walk.

"Your doctor called. He said he'll release you today if you like or you can stay one more night."

I knew Mark needed to be at work on Monday. If I wanted a nice, smooth ride in his SUV I'd have to check out today. Otherwise Jacob would have to come pick me up in his old Volvo station wagon the next morning.

I looked at Mark, who shrugged.

"It's up to you."

I knew the four-hour drive would be unpleasant either way but I decided to opt for the gentler ride.

"I think I'd like to be released today," I said.

"Okay, I'll get the paperwork ready." She started toward the door then paused. "Did you have a bowel movement yet, Ms. Edwards?"

"Uh, yes," I said, stretching the truth.

She tilted her chin toward her chest and looked over her glasses.

"A little," I said, doing my best to look completely earnest.

It was clear from her soft *hmmph* that she didn't believe me.

"I'll make sure we give you a scrip for stool softeners to take home with you."

As soon as she left, Mark spoke up.

"You're such a liar."

"A really bad one, apparently."

The ride home wasn't as bad as I'd expected, partly due to drugs and partly thanks to the pillow secured between my abdomen and the seat belt. To his credit, Mark would utter "bump!" each time he noted a potential bounce in the ride so I could brace myself with the cushion. When we reached Templeton he exited and drove to Trader Joe's.

"We need to fill your larder so you have enough food until Jacob can go out and get more. Wanna make a list?"

"I'd like to come in."

"Are you sure?"

"Yeah. I'm tired of being an invalid," I said, although I probably wouldn't be fooling anyone in my sweat pants and slippers.

He helped me out of the car and into the store where I used a cart to support myself, one hand across my belly to pad each step. By the time we reached the checkout the cart brimmed with easy-to-fix meals and plenty of fresh fruits and snacks. Mark refused to let me pay, gifting me with more than a week's worth of groceries.

"You're going to be out of a paycheck for a while," he said. "Let me get this."

When we turned onto my street and my house came into view I let out a sigh, relieved to finally be back. Mark pulled in the driveway and helped me into the house before retrieving the grocery bags. I crawled in bed while he put away the food.

"You've got water here on the nightstand, your phone's plugged in and charging next to it." He sat on the side of the bed. "Do you want a Vicodin?"

"Yeah, I think so."

He shook out a pill and handed me my water bottle.

"I need to head back to Monterey so I can get some sleep and be up early for a meeting tomorrow morning. When will

Jacob be home?"

"He's supposed to be here by ten tonight."

"I'm just a phone call away if you need anything. And you know that house full of girls next door would do anything for you."

"I know." I took his hand and kissed it. "Thank you. Thank you so much for everything. You're a really good friend."

"You're welcome. Now get some rest, okay?"

"Okay," I said.

I slept for most of the rest of the day except to shuffle to the bathroom and back to bed. When Jacob got home he ordered a *BBQ Bird* from Woodstock's Pizza and I surprised myself by eating two slices.

"I was thinking of meeting up with some friends later," Jacob said as he put the box in the fridge. "Is there anything you need between now and bedtime?"

"Actually, there is. I simply can't deal with this dirty hair for another minute. I can clean myself with a washcloth but would you help me shampoo my hair?"

"Of course," he said.

With a towel wrapped around my shoulders and a pillow held against my stomach, I leaned over the kitchen sink. My son tenderly lathered my hair then rinsed it with the sprayer. He worked some conditioner through my ends and sprayed again before wrapping the towel lopsidedly around my head.

"I can't tell you how much I appreciate that. I feel so much better."

He led me back to my bed and propped pillows behind me.

"No problem. You want me to bring you the blow dryer?"

"No, too tired," I said, running a wide toothed come through my fine hair.

"Well if you need me just send a text and I'll come back."

"I'll be okay and the girls are right next door."

"Promise me you won't do anything stupid like try to lift or move something. I know you."

"I promise," I said. "Go have some fun. You've worked hard this quarter and you deserve it."

He hugged me before heading back to his room.

After Jacob left I downed another Vicodin and closed my eyes, lost in gratitude for my life, my family, my friends, and my funky old house. I don't pray the way I used to but sometimes I talk to my mom and dad, finding comfort in their lingering presence in my life, long after their deaths. On this night I thanked them for not stopping at four children and for passing along good morals while acknowledging their imperfections.

And for giving me a couple of stellar kidneys to boot.

TWENTY-THREE

December 20, 2010 - February 2011

The hardest part of being home wasn't pain, but boredom. I'm used to being active, working hard, and taking care of the yard. Thankfully one of the girls from the house bought me a bed tray. This allowed me to stave off boredom by watching movies and surfing the Internet on my laptop between naps as I reclined in bed during my recuperation. A few friends stopped by with coffee or fresh veggie juice which also helped to break up the time.

Jacob made meals and did dishes, doing what he could to keep me comfortable and stop me from trying to do too much too soon. When his twenty-second birthday arrived a week after I returned home, I gave him a card with a $50 bill inside so he could go out and celebrate with friends.

"I know it's not much," I said, "but it's more than you had, right?"

He hugged me, careful not to squeeze too hard.

"Thanks, Mom. I really appreciate it."

"I appreciate you being so willing to help out this week."

He glanced up at the familiar stocking I'd hung before leaving for San Francisco a week earlier. We don't celebrate Christmas in a traditional way anymore except for the stocking, and he usually convinces me to let him empty it early. This year was no exception. It only took one *Please?* And I caved.

One by one he pulled out candies, an electric razor, and an assortment of unique items I'd collected throughout the year for the specific purpose of stuffing into his stocking. One year it was a straw you fit into your armpit and blow into that made fart sounds. This year it was a nose flute and when Jacob found it he bit into the fake lips and snorted into the opening. The sound that came out was not music but more like a *fffft-fffft-fffft* noise. He held it in place and looked at me.

"Hello, *Clarice*. I ate his liver with some fava beans and a nice Chianti. Fffftfffftfffftffffftfffft!"

"Stop! It still hurts to laugh!"

He set the nose horn aside and reached all the way into the toe to find the last object.

"Holy crap," he said, pulling out the box. "You got me an iPod Touch?"

A friend had given it to me to help pass my time while recuperating, but with money being tight the timing couldn't have been more perfect for re-gifting it to my son. He would certainly get a lot more use out of it.

"You'll use it?"

He carefully took the iPod out of the box and turned it on. The blue light reflected in his green eyes.

"Are you kidding? This is awesome!"

"I'm glad you like it."

He set the box aside and frowned.

"And this is where I feel terrible that I don't have gifts for you. I'm sorry. I'm soooo broke."

"All I want is for you to study hard and get good grades. Watching your graduation from UCSC will be the best gift you could ever give me."

"I'd do that anyway."

"If it makes you feel better you can make me some of your famous lemon bars tomorrow."

"I will, I promise."

"And you can take me to see *True Grit* on Christmas

Day."

"Done."

"Okay, then. Go have yourself a birthday."

He hugged me again.

"I love you, Mom."

"I love you, too. Happy birthday, Jacob."

He disappeared into his room to change his clothes. Through the wall I heard him squeak out a couple of notes on the nose flute. Knowing him, it was probably the theme song from *Silence of the Lambs*. Knowing me, I will never, ever watch that movie, no way, no how.

***

On Christmas morning I shuffled out to Jacob's Volvo and he drove us to Joe Momma's Coffee in Avila Beach. The owner and his family were serving free drinks to anyone who showed up between seven and ten on the holiday. The spa where I worked is situated on the mezzanine floor of the building and the coffee shop sits below on the street level. Not only had I missed my friends and co-workers during my recovery, I'd missed the fabulous coffee I'd become accustomed to drinking on a near-daily basis.

Michael, who happens to look a lot like Santa himself, was holding court with the last few customers in front of the coffee shop when we parked across the street. By the time we reached the door it was bolted. We put our faces to the glass and waved. Michael unlocked the door and welcomed us with his signature grin.

"Jacob!" He said, hugging my son. "How've you been?"

"I'm doing pretty well," he said. "Merry Christmas," he added.

Jacob chatted with the owner's son and daughter while we waited for our drinks. I managed to maneuver myself onto a stool and Michael brought me a slice of spinach quiche.

"I'm surprised to see you out and about already. You feeling pretty good?"

"It feels really good to get out," I said, taking a bite. "This is so yummy. Thank you."

"Merry Christmas," he said, and winked.

From the coffee shop Jacob and I drove south toward the movie theater where *True Grit* was playing. On the way it began pouring so hard the wipers could barely keep up with the rain. Jacob slowed down in response to my wide-eyed freaking out due to the passenger side blade not working.

"I can't see a thing," I said.

"I've got this," he said. "Relax."

I didn't relax but the more he drove the more I realized that he really was a safe driver and I needed to trust him. Unfortunately, thanks to getting a late start from Joe Momma's, we arrived just five minutes ahead of the movie start time. Jacob dropped me in front so I could get in line while he parked. As he walked up next to me the cashier taped a "Sorry, sold out" sign in the window.

"Aw, Mom," he said.

"Don't worry about it. I think I'm pushing it a little anyway."

"You sure? We can go get some lunch and come back for the next show."

"Let's try it another day," I said.

We drove home in the rain then played several games of Boggle, every one of which I lost.

"It's the drugs," I said. "I think my brain is still foggy."

"Is that the story you're going with?" he asked, as he boxed up the game.

"Stop gloating. You know I always win."

"*Used to* win," he said. "Hey, don't' blame me. You're the one that wanted me to study linguistics."

"Point taken."

He headed back to his room and within a few minutes I heard the low rumblings of Xbox battles. A soft knock sounded at the front door and I opened it to find one of my tenants.

"Hi, Ellie. I forgot to give this to you yesterday," she said, handing me an envelope. "It came in the mail for you yesterday."

"Thank you. I thought you all went home for the holidays."

"Everyone but me. I have to work."

"Aw, that's too bad."

"Not really," she said. "I'm glad to make the extra money. You feeling okay?"

"A little better each day. Thanks for asking."

"Merry Christmas, Ellie."

"Merry Christmas to you too, Honey."

The envelope was from my online journaling family with whom I'd been writing and sharing for over a decade. Inside were two $500 prepaid visa cards, along with a note.

Dear Ellie:

As you open this, I want you to imagine that all of us in Collective Journey are here in your home, sharing this time with you. We have all paused for a moment in our busy lives to salute and support you. Of course, we can't do this in real time but in our hearts, we are there with you in SLO.

We are in awe of the choices you have made to donate a kidney to a total stranger for no other reason than you have a healthy one, and he needs one. We would like to share in this adventure with you as part of our journaling group. In debating what to do, we decided the best way to support you would be to help with some of your expenses that you will incur as a part of your donation. We were thinking of your lost wages, since you will need time to recuperate and not be able to work.

Use these cards for whatever you need. Perhaps this will alleviate some of the stress that just naturally occurs when your income is curtailed. Know that we will be sharing this

*adventure with you and are hoping and praying for the best
outcome for all.*

*Lots of love to you,
All of your friends at Collective Journey*

I fingered the raised insignia on the Visa card, unable to hold
back tears. Feeling spent, I crawled into bed early and pulled
the covers to my chin. With the rain pummeling the skylight,
I lay silently as another Christmas came and went without
much hoopla. But with a heck of a lot of love.

***

Doctor Bry was right. Within a couple weeks following
surgery I needed only a couple of Tylenol for pain and I
moved around more easily. I continued to feel better and
couldn't wait to get back to work, but I needed a release from
the doctors. My driving privileges hadn't yet been granted
and Jacob had returned to Santa Cruz. Fortunately, Nick
happened to be headed to Northern California for a retreat the
day before my follow-up appointment. He brought me to the
Kabuki in San Francisco where I would once again stay
overnight after my exam at CPMC.

I checked in at the hotel desk, then caught the first
shuttle to the transplant center. A doctor I'd never met took
less than thirty seconds to tell me what I already knew.

"Everything looks good. No infection, swelling is down.
We'll see you again in about three months."

"Is it odd that I've lost nine pounds since the surgery?"

"Does it bother you?" he asked, pausing in the doorway.

"No. I needed to lose a few pounds."

"Then I'm not concerned, either."

When I returned to the reception area Lana handed me a
small box that held a plated sterling silver star on a key
chain. *Because you're a star*, read the note inside.

"I know it's not much and legally we're not allowed to

gift anything of value to a patient but it's our small way of saying how grateful we are for your donation."

"Thank you," I said. "It's really pretty."

I asked Lana if she'd heard anything from the recipient. He'd still not replied to my letter and although I wanted to respect his privacy I was a little disappointed that he hadn't made contact.

"The last I heard he was doing well," she assured me, "but I'll check in again with the team in New Jersey. "

"I'd really appreciate that Lana."

***

My good friend Julienne happened to be driving to Los Angeles from Northern California the next morning and had offered to give me a lift home instead of taking the train. We'd planned ahead to meet at the Kabuki after my appointment so we could hang out for the evening. She'd moved to Ukiah a few years back and I'd missed her terribly.

I met Julienne by accident. I'd walked into her salon next to one of my favorite coffee houses on a whim and asked if there was anyone who might specialize in fine hair. She sat me in her chair and gave me the best scalp massage I'd ever had while explaining what she thought would look good with my face structure.

"Man," I said, "At this point you can do just about anything you want. You sure do give good head."

She burst out laughing. We spent the next couple of hours trading life stories, talking about our kids, and realizing we were long-lost sisters, destined to meet. As it turned out we had a lot in common, from serial marriages to moving around often, to very similar upbringings. Both our young lives had been heavily influenced by men who ruled from behind a heavy curtain of theology. Our fathers were religiously strict men whom we loved deeply, yet as is often the case, we'd walked away from their righteousness in our teens to begin a private search for that which is sacred. We couldn't know then that we would someday recognize it in each other. And find it within ourselves.

For a time I'd swapped my Old Time religion for New Age beliefs but eventually discarded both ideologies in favor of angels who are here, right now, in human form. Lots of girlfriends have come and gone in the last forty years and only three or four have remained steadfast in our love for one another regardless of time, distance, or the interweave of romantic relationships. Julienne is one of them. To reach for her in my darkest moments and feel her loving presence is to touch the face of God. I completely respect others' beliefs but I'll take that soft human cheek, that warm hand, that soothing voice over full chakras or an empty tomb any day.

I heard her before I saw her sprinting toward me on the sidewalk, bracelets jangling as she ran.

"Ellie!"

"Jules!" I squealed, not running because I still couldn't manage much more than a medium-fast walk.

We threw our arms around each other in front of the hotel, tilting side to side like a couple of metronomes in three-quarter time.

"You look great!" she said, stepping away to eye me from head to toe, then back to head. I imagined she probably wished she had a pair of shears in her pocket. I'd not found a decent hairdresser since she'd moved away and had taken to wearing stubby pink pigtails under my fine, blond hair, that I'd (obviously, to her) been trimming myself. "How do you feel?"

"Pretty good, actually. I'm so glad you were headed to L.A. I've missed you so much."

"I've missed you too, Ellie."

Her phone pinged and she reached into her bag to check a text message then tossed it back in.

"Hey, are you hungry? I heard about this great Vietnamese place with fabulous pho."

"Starving," I said." Probably not up to dancing but dinner and a movie sounds good. Since you picked the food, I choose *The King's Speech*."

"Perfect!" she said, grabbing my hand. "The restaurant is only about twelve blocks from here."

"Okay, but you're going to have to slow it down a bit."

"Oh, sorry Ellie. I already forgot."

"No worries. Let's just take it a little slower."

We never made it to the Vietnamese restaurant. We got lost and ended up eating at one of the sushi places in Japantown where we feasted on edamame and soup, then stuffed ourselves on popcorn at the nearby theater. By the time we made it back to the hotel I was exhausted but thrilled to have reconnected with my girlfriend, whom I had dearly missed.

The next day Jules dropped me off at my house after a four hour drive through heavy traffic. We hugged in the driveway and I promised I'd try to get up to Ukiah for a visit one day soon. As she sped off toward the 101 I instinctively put my hand on my heart as I often do when friends leave. I'm not sure if it's a way of blessing them or blessing me but for some reason it brings me comfort.

After unpacking my bags I opened my computer to find an email from Lana waiting for me.

Dear Eldonna:

It was good to see you looking so well today. I checked with the East Coast hospital and it seems they never received your card. If you'd like to email me the letter I'll reprint it and forward it to them again. I'm so sorry for the mix-up!

All the best,
Lana

Not having heard any response from the recipient I'd worried that the kidney had failed and they were just protecting me from the news. On one hand, it was almost better not knowing the outcome. However, now that I knew my recipient never received my communication I found myself hopeful again. From the beginning I'd had a good feeling about the successful outcome of my donation. After reading Lana's note I felt more optimistic that I'd receive news of my recipient's continued good health even if it wasn't directly from him.

***

Three and a half weeks after surgery I returned to work. Not a lot and not with any deep-tissue clients but I knew in my heart of hearts that my body was ready and my spirit was more than prepared. There's something about giving a massage that circles around through the receiver and back to the giver. I'm constantly telling my clients that you can't give from an empty well but what they might not realize is how they fill me up merely by their presence on my table.

Near the end of my first week back to work I made another appearance on Dave Congalton's radio show to talk about the transplant process. I still ached for Kathy and Jim and I wanted to once again ask listeners to consider being tested. Unfortunately, most of the calls we got that day were from people who couldn't understand why anyone would donate an organ. I was afraid my efforts had backfired and these folks had scared off anyone who might have made the call I was hoping for. Even Dave commented that although he'd be fine giving away organs after he dies, the idea of donating while he's still alive remains disconcerting.

No matter how hard I try to communicate the need for donors, people remain skeptical. No matter how deeply I underscore the extraordinary sense of purpose in helping another human being, I continually bump up against fear. What I've gradually come to understand is that it's naïve to presume anyone's motivations for donating or not, other than my own.

Whenever I felt melancholy about Kathy, I'd remind myself that I did the right thing at the right time and in the way that seemed most sensible, given my age and the improbability of finding a donor for someone as difficult to match as Kathy. However, this realization didn't stop me from continuing my mission. I decided to reach out one more time on Facebook to see if any friends or their friends might consider being tested. I was halfway through creating the post when a *new message* icon popped up at the top of the screen. I tried to ignore it so I could finish my quest but curiosity got the best of me and I clicked over to my mailbox. When I read the heading I felt a rush of giddiness and apprehension:

Are you my kidney donor?

TWENTY-FOUR

2011

Turns out his name isn't Frankie, it's Mike. His message read simply: *Lives in California and grew up in Michigan. Sounds like you.*

I answered that yes, I was indeed his donor and asked how he was feeling. He replied a few hours later.

I went over your Facebook entries and it was kind of surreal reading what felt like your journal on the days leading up to the transplant and then to listen to the podcast of your story on the radio. Thank you for not having an average name. I'm doing fine; I was in and out of the hospital in four days. Your kidney is a non-stop urine machine! I was going to ask how you are doing but I just listened to the podcast of your radio interview.

I started writing you a letter and a card and thought why not see if I can find her on Facebook? I've been dealing with kidney failure for 18 years. Did dialysis for 5 years and got a transplant. That lasted 12 years and I started dialysis again in October so I wasn't on it that long this time. I was going to ask you a bunch of questions but you answered them all in the radio interview. Is there anything you would like to know?

He had me at *non-stop urine machine*. The miracle of

technology had allowed two strangers to be matched for organ transplantation without one ever having met the other. Thanks to social media we could see each other's photos and exchange information. But other than knowing his name, where he lived, and that his wife had donated so that he'd be eligible for a non-directed kidney, I knew almost nothing about him. I had so many questions I hardly knew where to start.

Hi Mike! It's great to hear from you and I'm glad your new kidney is working like a champ. Do you notice a difference between this transplant and your first one? How is your wife doing? Do you know how the woman in Chicago is doing or if there were any more down the line after her? I keep hearing about all the snowstorms on the East Coast and in the Midwest. I admit I do not miss the weather. Thanks for looking me up on Facebook. I've gone from completely silent about the transplant to full-on spokesperson for living donation. Since I can't donate any more kidneys my new goal is to get as many other people to sign up as possible. ~~Ellie

In his next email I learned that Mike's protein levels were already normal—something he never expected to see again—and that his wife was recovering well. Her kidney went to a twenty eight year-old patient in Chicago who'd been on dialysis since childhood. They didn't know if the chain continued beyond that.

Mike also shared that he was not someone who thrived on dialysis and had been considering bringing in hospice.

Almost two decades of being involved with this gets to you after awhile. Thanks to you I will be rockin and rollin for at least another decade! I will always greatly appreciate what you did for me especially not knowing who was going to get it. It is something you should always be proud of. Everything is normal in my life because of you. I somehow don't think, "Thanks for the kidney" quite does it. ~~Mike

Maybe not for him but it did it for me. I just felt so relieved to hear directly from Mike that he was well, his wife was well, and that the kidney was doing its job so well. In fact, not only was his new organ as functional in him as it had been in me, he noted that he'd lost his taste for foods he normally craved like lamb and ice cream, foods I'd never liked.

Of course I totally stalked his Facebook profile. He'd posted very few photos of himself and used Jack Nicholson's iconic image from *The Shining* as a profile picture, which I found a bit unsettling. I did discover one recent photo which showed a round-faced man with reddish hair but he wore sunglasses so I couldn't see his eyes. In another, a younger version of Mike stood on a beach smiling at his beautiful wife who held a colorful parasol. They looked truly happy.

As I scrolled through his liked groups and Facebook pages another thing became obvious: Mike and I couldn't be more politically diverse. When I'd said earlier that I hoped my age limit ruled out Dick Cheney, it was as if the universe decided I needed to learn a lesson about what it really means to give with a warm hand. In contrast to my Rachael Maddow, Jon Stewart, and Obama 2012 pages, he subscribed to "Defend Assault Weapons," "I Did Not Vote for Obama" and "Tea Party Patriots" groups. I could almost see the gods rolling on their backs, their feet kicking in the air, gasping for breath between howls of laughter.

At first, I admit it, I was a little stunned. But after seeing pictures of his wife and family, reading comments from friends cheering him on and wishing him well—many offering blessings to me, his unknown donor—the initial feelings of disappointment simply dissipated. What became clear was that just like me, Mike has a family and friends who love him. Our differences in politics or values don't need to separate us. In fact, this diversity is exactly what unites us as unique individuals. We're each of us just people trying to survive and do our best in this life.

Dear Mike,

This has been such an incredible journey. You have no idea the gift you have given back to me by being part of it. I've learned so much about kidney disease and the daunting lack of donors as well as the miserable hours upon hours of dialysis that kidney patients must endure. Please take good care of yourself and know that you have a friend rooting for you on the left coast.

All Best, Ellie

PS: Let me know if you suddenly have the urge to write checks to Greenpeace or show up at war protests. <grin>

Over the next few months Mike and I exchanged several emails and learned more about each other's journey up to this point. He'd begun affectionately referring to me as his hippie chick. I told him about Kathy and he told me about the sister who'd donated the kidney that had kept him alive for the previous dozen years. Reading his letters moved me more than I can easily express. Knowing that he was thriving after being so close to calling it quits left me feeling both awed and stunned.

Shortly after hearing from Mike I did something I've never done before nor ever expected to. An hour after entering a local tattoo shop I left with an inked row of tiny pink flowers along the side of my right foot and a lotus above my heel: the symbol of rebirth rising from murky water. Author and philosopher Ralph W. Trine once wrote, "Love is everything. It is the key to life, and its influences are those that move the world." I shortened the quote on the top of my foot to the first three words. The rest, to me, is self evident.

***

Almost a year after my donation I made a return visit to Dave's radio show, along with a seventy-six year old kidney patient who was getting desperate. Dave had invited me to answer questions and address concerns from any potential donors who might call in.

"Have you noticed anything different since donating?" Dave asked, before opening the phone lines.

"Yeah. I've lost 25 pounds and I feel fantastic."

"So you'd do it again?"

"In a heartbeat. If I had three kidneys I give away another one."

A man called in to challenge Dave's elderly guest, insisting he'd lived a good, long life.

"Who are you to take a kidney from someone younger who might need it?" he asked.

"Who are you to play God?" The older man responded.

When the debate heated up I buried myself in scribbled notes until I heard Dave announce, "We have Mike from New Jersey on the line."

I cupped the headphones with my hands and pressed them to my ears.

"Oh my God. *Mike*?"

"Yeah, this is the guy walking around with your kidney."

Tears stung the corners of my eyes as my recipient revealed that he'd just come from the doctor and his kidney was functioning better than a person his age without kidney disease. I heard Boston with bits of New Jersey riding between the deep tones of his voice but the words themselves started to blur as I broke down. Dave asked Mike to stay on hold as he cut to commercial.

He handed me a box of tissues and squeezed my shoulder.

"Pull yourself together, dear. We've only got a couple minutes before we come back on."

Dave returned to his spot behind the microphone and slipped his headphones back on.

"Is there anything you'd like to say to Ellie," he asked Mike when we were live again.

"Thank you? I don't know. I get a little filled up when I talk about it."

Mike's voice cracked a bit and Dave thanked him for calling in. I don't remember much of the conversation that went on between Dave's other guest and callers, or even my own comments for the rest of the segment. I kept hearing Mike's voice in my ears saying, *one hundred percent kidney function* and I would choke up again.

At the end of the hour Dave asked his ailing guest if he had any last words.

The desperate man leaned into the microphone, his head turned slightly toward me. Behind us, his wife watched silently from behind a glass door as he spoke.

"I just hope there are more Ellies out there."

There are. I know there are. Perhaps you, reading these words, right now. Maybe not today, maybe not tomorrow, but if my story has planted a seed, if just one person asks, *If not me, then who?* I will have accomplished what I set out to do in sharing this journey with you. Twenty-four kidney patients were added to the UNOS list in the approximate time it took you to read this book, bringing the total to over ninety-seven thousand people who will die without a transplant.

One of them is waiting to hear from for you.

EPILOGUE

Three years after my donation I continue to feel fabulous. In what I like to refer to as instant karma, I became stronger and more fit post-transplant. The weight loss along with the greater sense of purpose one enjoys after donating has convinced me that it was one of the best decisions I've ever made in my life. Friends often comment on how happy I seem. I am. Not that I was unhappy before but I can't begin to describe the euphoria that accompanies becoming a living donor. I've heard similar statements from others who have donated. Everyone experiences varied outcomes but I can only liken my heightened sense of peace to the bliss many women feel after the birth of a child.

In July of 2012 I got an early morning call from Kathy.

"I'm on my way to San Francisco," she said through sobs. "I'm getting a kidney."

Her donor had technically died but the hospital was keeping the woman on life support because the family had chosen to donate her organs. It was a loving act during what must have been a horrific time for them. And yet I like to think they take comfort in the fact that Kathy is alive and thriving as a result of their decision.

When I first decided to donate I didn't talk about it much because I felt uncomfortable when people would gush about what a great thing I was planning to do. If I needed time off for example, I'd just say it was for some general tests or that I was having elective surgery. But eventually I realized if I didn't talk about it, how would I ever begin to challenge others to consider living donation? Now, instead of changing the subject I just thank people as graciously as possible and ask if they've signed up to be a donor on their driver's licenses. If they say no, I refer them to www.donatelife.net to register as an organ donor when they die. If they're curious about *living* donation I send them to www.kidneyregistry.org or www.lkdn.org.

If you're considering the idea of becoming a living donor I encourage you to contact the nearest transplant facility and offer to be tested. The hospital will give you a good idea of what to expect as well as being able to make sure that you wouldn't be compromising your own health. You can find a list of transplant centers and tons of information about the donation process at the above websites. Facebook also offers several forums where living donors answer questions from those interested in the process, including financial resources, emotional support, and post-op recovery.

Not only did I become more vocal about becoming a living donor, I offered to allow a documentary filmmaker to follow my journey, recording everything from driving lessons with my son, to doing massage, to filming the actual surgery. *Perfect Strangers* is currently making the festival circuit and will hopefully reach a wider audience as time progresses. Sharing such an intimate part of my life was a surreal experience but director Jan Krawitz made it seem effortless and I often forgot her crew was even in the room.

Like many other mid-lifers on the verge of an empty nest, I'd decided to go back to school to reignite sluggish synapses and broaden my knowledge base. I don't think any of us roll out of bed, slug back a cup of coffee, and suddenly decide this is the day we're going to dangle our ordinary little life by its ankles. I never dreamt that meeting a particular student in a gender studies class would teach me more than I could ever hope to learn in a book or a lecture, or change my life in such a powerful way.

Organ donation might seem like a big deal to a lot of people but every day I come across others who are doing or have done things I could never do. People who've adopted a special needs child, for example. People who commit their lives to aiding homeless refugees or teaching impoverished folks in inner cities. Sometimes just getting up in the morning on those days you barely feel human and doing whatever it takes to feed the kids and get them off to school requires an act of valor. Heroism is merely love in action. And in the end, love really is *everything*...

ACKNOWLEDGMENTS

I am so grateful for the amazing people in my life who helped to make this book a reality. From Kathy and Jim who allowed me into their lives, to my dear friend and medical advocate, Mark, to the doctors and nurses to all the folks I met as a result of beginning this amazing journey, thank you. This story belongs to you.

Writing is mostly a solo process but turning one's words into a publishable body of work is very much a collaborative effort. A shout-out to my online writing group *Collective Journey* who has provided a bounty of creative, spiritual, and personal support over the last fifteen years. Thanks to my beta readers, most especially the beautiful, smart, and funny Barbara Ristine Howard who took her red pen to the manuscript and made it bleed in all the right places. Thanks also to Dave Congalton for his advocacy for writers and enthusiastic support of this project. An ocean of thanks to Stan for your faith in my writing abilities and backing it up with tangible actions. And a special thank you to my son Jacob for not only putting up with a mom who writes but for providing all the best lines.

Finally, my deepest gratitude goes to my ineffable friend and companion Brer, who painstakingly helped me shape a rough draft into a complete and cohesive story. The Great Comma Slaughter of 2013 will leave its mark on my writing for years to come. Without your hours upon hours of patience, kind direction, irreverent humor and our shared devotion to language this book would have been a hundred times harder to finish. I love you so much.

HOW A TRANSPLANT CHAIN WORKS*

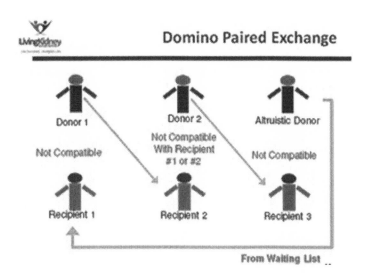

A domino paired kidney exchange starts with a non-directed or altruistic donor. Instead of just one person benefiting from their donation, this donor can allow many incompatible pairs to be transplanted.

Graphic printed with permission from Living Kidney Donors Network.

THE ENGLISH PAPER THAT STARTED IT ALL

Research Prospectus

Tentative / Claim

Seventeen people die every day in the US while waiting for an available transplant organ. Encouraging doctors and medical institutions to accept organs from altruistic donors not only addresses the lack of available organs but impacts the financial, emotional, and physical well-being of individuals, families, and our society as a whole. The basis for my claim will be proven through statistics, survival rates, and personal interviews with patients and donors that dispute claims of abuse by transplant advocates and hidden motives on the part of non-directed donors.

What do you already know about the topic?

Many hospitals and medical centers refuse to perform transplant surgery between a patient and an altruistic donor, citing ethical concerns. In gathering preliminary research, I've found organizations that pair patients with strangers with great success. Also, there are a lot of myths associated with organ donation, and experience has taught me that when people are educated they will more readily open their minds to facts.

What don't you know?

I want to bring this issue down to the local level. I don't know what percentage of people currently are registered donors or how to go about disseminating information that would encourage people to donate their organs. I don't know if Cuesta College would allow me to present such a program or would support my efforts to educate students.

Where will you start to find what you don't know?

I plan to check the UNOS website for statistics. I've already called the National Kidney Foundation and they're sending me a packet of material. I'll need to approach college administration to ask for their support/participation. I might also contact the local dialysis centers to interview patients.

How can I help you?

Cut me some slack on the draft deadlines as I changed topics midstream...

Eldonna Edwards
Fleming/English 1A

Body of Influence: The Case for Altruistic Organ Donation

On the morning of January 3, 2007 Wesley Autrey waited with his children on a platform alongside thousands of other commuters in New York City's Grand Central Station. Moments ahead of an oncoming train he shoved his two young daughters toward a middle-aged woman before jumping onto the tracks. Bystanders screamed as the construction worker curled himself around a convulsing young man, pushing his head into an odiferous soup of mud and sewage before flattening his own body like a shield as the train roared over the two of them. Amazingly, both men survived.

Although random acts of kindness don't always make national headlines Mr. Autrey is not an anomaly. Huge numbers of Good Samaritans are willing to take an informed risk in order to save the life of a dying stranger via living organ donation. However, thousands of patients die unnecessarily every year in the U.S. because surgeons and hospitals that provide organ transplant services often prohibit altruistic donors from participating in organ transplantation, quoting ethical reasons for the denial of non-related organ donation. This prohibitive practice flies in the face of common sense and logic when altruistic donors, by virtue of their compassionate nature and a lesser emotional investment in outcome, make better organ donors than relatives or friends. In addition, by welcoming and even encouraging altruistic organ donation, transplant teams effectually remove patients from the national waiting list, thereby reducing the wait for other, possibly needier, transplant candidates.

As organ transplant procedures improve and long-term

success continues to rise, transplant professionals are faced with creating policy that addresses the ethical issues involving the transfer of living tissue from one human being to another. In 2003, several authors collaborated in the "At Issue" series published by *GreenHaven Press* to debate the controversial aspects of organ transplantation. In the Introduction to *Organ Transplants*, Editor James D. Torr writes, "The field of organ transplantation is one of the miracles of modern medicine but its power to save lives depends directly on the availability of organs" (12). Yet despite the obvious need for organs, many medical professionals continue to adopt policies that preclude altruistic donors—a policy sociologists like Keiran Healy find objectionable. In his 2006 book, *Last Best Gifts: Altruism and the Market for Human Blood and Organs*, Healy states, "We must get away from the character and motives of individual donors and look instead to the cultural contexts and organizational mechanisms that provide people with reasons and opportunities to give" (2).

In order to better understand the need for changes in the rules as they apply to potential living donors, one must first grasp the over-reaching need for organs and the vast gap in organ availability. As of the date of this writing, over 96,000 candidates are currently on the OPTN (Organ Procurement and Transplant Network) waiting list. Last year, less than a third of that number received one or more organ transplants (many patients receive multiple organs such as kidney and pancreas) and approximately 6,700 died while waiting for a needed transplant, according to The United Network for Organ Sharing, or UNOS, which was established in 1984 as a non-profit organization for the purpose of developing a database system for the collection, storage, analysis and publication of all OPTN data pertaining to the patient waiting list, organ matching, and transplants.

Obviously, there are more patients awaiting a needed organ than there are available donors, living or dead, to fill that need. In 1984, the United States government passed the National Organ Transplant Act, which, among other things pertaining to organ procurement mechanisms, outlaws the sale of human organs, after ads for needed organs began appearing in newspapers offering to pay willing donors. In addition to the prevention of an open market for human organs, one more reason for the lack of available organs is the current policy many surgeons, hospitals, and transplant teams have endorsed which prevents altruistic (non-related) living donors from participation in the transplant process. Given the huge discrepancy between registered patients and available organs, it would seem obvious that transplant centers and surgical teams would welcome altruistic donors in order to save more lives.

Unfortunately, this is not the case. In July of 2005, NATCO, The Organization for Transplant Professionals, adopted a Policy Statement from *The Program for Transplant Policy and Ethics*, which states:

Donor families who respond to solicitation undoubtedly believe that they are altruistic and helping someone in need; however, in effect, donor families are unwittingly hurting the chances of the patients most in need by preventing those patients at the top of the list from receiving an organ. The public is generally unaware of the consequences organ solicitation has for the many others awaiting an organ transplant. The portrayal of the personal heart-wrenching stories of an individual in need is powerful. So the public watches with a sympathetic eye to those who are soliciting an organ, often not knowing the dire consequences to others on the list.

NATCO proposes that under no circumstance will solicitation for organs from either living or deceased donors be permitted. Commercial solicitation is especially reprehensible and should be stopped. Organs obtained by patients through solicitation should not be transplanted. Policy should be written and enacted to stop solicitation and to prevent solicited organs from being transplanted. Organizations that require "members" to donate organs, either living or deceased, to a selected group, bypassing the UNOS allocation, should not be permitted to exist.

In their conclusion, this committee assumes that altruistic donors somehow rob patients currently on the waiting list their entitlement to be next in line. This conclusion is faulty, based upon current provisions wherein a wife may donate a kidney to her husband even if he is not at the top of the list. Applying the logic of the above policy statement, the authors would infer that a donor-wife is somehow precluding the top-listed patient on the UNOS registry of an implied right to her kidney instead of her beloved mate when it is quite likely the wife wouldn't be donating a kidney if not for her loving connection to her spouse. Likewise, folks who become aware of a patient on a donor-matching registry outside of UNOS designed to attract potential organ donors often do so because they feel a connection to a particular patient on the list. The potential donor might very well have altruistic motives but just like the wife who donates a kidney to her husband, the donation is often an act of enlightened self-interest.

To their credit, UNOS, according to an article last year by Barbara Basler and Chad Hudnall published in the *AARP Bulletin*, "is considering a national registry of live donors that could dramatically increase kidney transplants in America. But it will take action by Congress to do so. The registry would list patients along with their friends and relatives who wanted to donate a kidney but were not a match. Patients across the country could "swap" one of their donors who doesn't match for a donor who does" (15).

Basler and Hudnall also report that skeptics claim the practice of web solicitation for donors "undermines the current organ donation and allocation system by giving those with more money, Internet savvy, the most heart-wrenching story and even the cutest picture an edge over those who might be sicker but poorer, less resourceful, less sympathetic or just less photogenic" (16). In truth, thanks to public libraries, just about anyone has access to the web. Also, nonprofit donor-matching organizations use the registration income to run their sites, and often waive fees for those who cannot afford a listing. Finally, any potential donor who asks for money is immediately banned from respected sites and registered donors' ads are carefully screened for any hint of underlying financial motives.

Contrary to skeptics' concerns, I am a perfect example of the above "altruistic" donor who is thankful that the Internet provided me access to real people with real stories. I first chose to donate my kidney upon hearing of a student with renal disease. In truth, I would not likely have been inclined to have my abdomen cut open and an organ removed had I not felt good about keeping this bright, young woman alive. After all, she is a feminist, an environmentalist, and a shining example of what it means to live lightly on the planet—all values I share. Although this student turned down my offer (for reasons pertaining to her beliefs about overpopulation and Darwinism), once I had been exposed to the need for living donors, I began actively seeking a patient-matching registry on the Internet. Among the list of candidates, I was drawn to a woman named Kathy on the Matching Donors website who is a few years older than me who is a Hospice nurse and a new grandmother. When I asked my potential organ recipient why she'd chosen to advertise on the website, she told me her chances of getting to the top of the UNOS list before her disease made it impossible to enjoy life was slim to none. A quick check of the OPTN resource data backs up her summation. Currently over 15,500 kidney candidates are registered with UNOS in California alone yet less than 2,000 them will receive a transplanted organ in 2007. Of those, 75 percent will have been waiting for five or more years.

The act of offering a kidney to a woman I've never met

indeed mirrors my altruistic nature, however, it is fair to say I would not have felt as strongly about undergoing major surgery for a completely unknown patient (known as non-directed donation). Also, had it not been for the opportunity to read patients' histories in their own words, I might not have even registered as a donor, thereby disproving NATCO's underlying motivations for a prohibiting donors like me who they imply would have given my kidney to whomever is at the top of the waiting list.

Altruism, as defined by sociologist Roberta Simmons in her article, "Altruism and Sociology" published in the *Sociological Quarterly* "(1) seeks to increase another's welfare, not one's own; (2) is voluntary; (3) is intentional, meant to help someone else; and (4) expects no external reward" (2-3). Given the fact that the sale of organs is illegal, policy makers who prohibit altruistic organ donation are engaging in a practice that is not only a great disservice to their patients, but could have major negative consequences. In swearing to the Hippocratic Oath to uphold ethical standards in their practice of medicine, physicians promise to "...apply, for the benefit of the sick, all measures [that] are required, avoiding those twin traps of over-treatment and therapeutic nihilism" (Lasagna—3:2). Refusing transplant surgery based upon misguided ethics harms those who would benefit from altruistic donations, possibly to a mortal degree. Altruistic living donors do not rob needy patients any more than relatives of low-listed patients do, and in fact, effectually remove patients from the list allowing others to rise to the top more quickly.

Altruistic donors also make better donor candidates because they have less emotional investment in the outcome than related donors. Imagine if our hero in the New York Subway had known the young man struggling on the tracks. What if it had been his child, his brother, or his wife convulsing in the mud? And what if, despite his heroic efforts, that relative had died or suffered serious injuries?

Would he have been as apt to appear on camera, tell his story, and accept a check from a wealthy philanthropist? I don't think he would have because his emotional investment in the outcome would have been much greater and he would be mourning his failure. In fact, he may not even have jumped (or jumped too late) because his thought process would have taken longer to distill action through a filter of love and panic and possible heartbreak—a filter that would consume precious seconds before the train roared by.

This implied guilt-factor is exactly why doctors are not ethically allowed to treat family members. Who would argue that the inability to save a loved one through the trained precision of your own knife wouldn't have a much greater impact than if an objective, reputable surgeon performed the needed surgery? Why is it then that the opposite rule is applied to altruistic organ donors? Wouldn't it make more sense to accommodate donors who have little emotional investment in the outcome of organ donation other than knowing they have contributed to the possible well-being of another over guilt-ridden—possibly even coerced— relatives of the patient? Similarly, what if a sign had been posted in the subway station prohibiting anyone from jumping onto the tracks to save another? Would Mr. Autry have hesitated or would he have jumped anyway? I believe he would have, because Mr. Autrey's inherent compassion for another human being would have trumped rules meant to protect his own safety. According to an article in *The New York Times*, when asked why he would risk his life to help a stranger in such a dangerous situation, he simply replied, "I don't feel like I did something spectacular; I just saw someone who needed help. I did what I felt was right."

Everybody—especially Americans—loves a hero. The day after Navy veteran Wesley Autrey rescued the young man struggling on the train tracks, he was paraded from talk show to talk show to discuss his selfless act of courage. It's no surprise that Mr. Autrey's quick-thinking action culminated in a significant check from a generous benefactor who wanted to reward what he believed was a rare act of kindness toward a complete stranger. People all over the country and beyond applauded the man's bravery with letters and accolades. However, if you watched closely, you would see this humble new hero's embarrassment and discomfort with all the attention. Mr. Autrey didn't do what he did to gain notoriety or reward; he did it because it needed doing, and nobody else in the crowd was acting on that need.

In the film, *Freedom Writers*, an inner city teen asks Miep Gies, Anne Frank's protector during World War II, why she took such a great risk to protect the young girl and her family. Ms. Gies answers, "I did what I had to do because it is the right thing to do, that is all. [Anyone], even a teenager, can turn on a small light in a dark room."

Like Ms. Gies, Mr. Autrey responded to need in the same way people choose to take action when a creek is being polluted, a child is abused, or someone is unnecessarily dying due to the lack of available organ donors. Unfortunately, current transplant policy not only cripples the intention of a democratic society in which people retain the right to their bodies, it alters the possibilities in outcome for people in situations like the young man on the tracks, who certainly would have died if not for the freedom of a compassionate father to act on his values toward human life. For many, taking action is not merely an opportunity to do good, it is a moral obligation in the interest of our planet's health and hope for its inhabitants' continued humanity toward their fellow beings.

WORKS CITED

Basler, Barbara, and Chad Hudnall. "Winning the Waiting Game." <u>AARP Bulletin</u> June 2006: 14-16.

Buckley, Cara. "Man is Rescued by Stranger on Subway Tracks." <u>New York Times</u>

3 Jan. 2007. 19 May 2007 <http://www.nytimes.com/2007/01/03/nyregion/03life.htm?ex=1179720000&en=4aa57c91bd2b1970&ei=5070>.

"Donation Facts and Statistics." <u>Donor Awareness Council</u>. 2006. 12 May 2007 < http://www.donor-awareness.org/info.facts.html>.

"Fast Facts About Transplant." <u>Scientific Registry of Transplant Recipients</u>. 2007. 19

May 2007 <http://www.ustransplant.org/csr/current/fastfacts.aspx>.

Gruters, Ginger A., M.A. "Living Donors: Process, Outcomes, and Ethical Questions."
    <u>The President's Council on Bioethics</u>. Sept. 2006. 19 May 2007

<http://www.bioethics.gov/background/ginger_gruters.html>.

<u>Freedom Writers</u>. Dir. Richard LaGravenese. Perf. Hilary Swank, Patrick Dempsey.

DVD. Paramount Pictures, 2006.

Healy, Kieran. Last Best Gifts: Altruism and the Market for Human Blood and Organs.

University of Chicago Press, 2006.

Lasagna, Louis. The Lasagna Oath. Ms. 3:2. Rochester University Library, New York.

1964.

Simmons, Roberta G. "Altruism and Sociology." Sociological Quarterly 32nd ser. (1991):

1-22.

Stein, Rob. "Search for Transplant Organs Becomes a Web Free-for-All." Washington

Post 23 Sept. 2005, sec. A: 01+.

Torr, James D., ed. At Issue: Organ Transplants. 1st ed. San Diego: GreenHaven P, 2003.

9-12.

"25 Facts About Organ Donation and Transplantation." National Kidney Foundation.

2007. 19 May 2007 <http://www.kidney.org>.

"Understanding Donation." DonateLife America. 2006. 19 May 2007

<http://www.shareyourlife.org/understandingdonation>.

"Organ Donation and Transplantation Data." United
Network for Organ Sharing. May

2007. Organ Procurement and Transplantation Network.
19 May 2007

<http://unos.org/data/>.

Wheeler, Kathy. Telephone interview. 1 May 2007.

Made in the USA
Columbia, SC
26 January 2018